My Way

One Nurse's Passion for End of Life

JOY NUGENT

BALBOA.PRESS
A DIVISION OF HAY HOUSE

Balboa Press books may be ordered through booksellers or by contacting:

Balboa Press
A Division of Hay House
1663 Liberty Drive
Bloomington, IN 47403
www.balboapress.com
AU TFN: 1 800 844 925 (Toll Free inside Australia)
AU Local: 0283 107 086 (+61 2 8310 7086 from outside Australia)

The photograph on the front cover is of the author and one of her patients. It was taken on her camera in 1992 and is shared with her permission and permission of the patient's family.

Print information available on the last page.

ISBN: 978-1-5043-1199-1 (sc)
ISBN: 978-1-5043-2341-3 (hc)
ISBN: 978-1-5043-1200-4 (e)

Balboa Press rev. date: 11/11/2020

CONTENTS

FOREWORD

What led me to become a nurse? It is a long story. I was born in beautiful countryside—a mountain-framed setting where pineapples grew in neat rows and avocados and other fruit grew in a natural valley blessed with rich top soil and sufficient rain. Even when I was a child, significant dreams came to me as if with a message. The first childhood dream was a recurring nightmare in which I saw a knife on a flight of stairs leading up to the front door of the home my parents built when they married. Years later, and in sessions of hypnosis which lasted over thirty hours, I saw a little three-year-old girl looking sad and bewildered, and I understood the meaning of that dream. When I was a three-year-old child, I received my first wounding.

Some youths had visited the farm and thought it funny to torment my little-girl self and to wound her tiny vagina with a stick. I remember it hurt for a long time when I sat on my pot to pee. It never occurred to me to tell my parents who were busy doing "good" in their own worlds. I buried the event in my unconscious until it was brought to light during my midlife by an understanding doctor who practised hypnotherapy. In 2013, I was to gain a diploma in clinical hypnosis, and I used this therapy in the process of being a midwife to souls who were leaving a no-longer-useful body. For many years, I have had the desire to understand the unconscious and to gain access to the guidance which comes from the different levels of consciousness. My understanding is that the dream state is the interface between this world and the next.

Following my thirty hours of hypnosis, and in my midlife, I was able to comfort that small child and to say to her that, while bad things happen in life, they do not define us. A short time after the wounding from those thoughtless youths, I was to receive another lesson that, in an unconscious way, led to my profession as a palliative care nurse and the birth of compassion. It was my father's habit to drown the kittens my mummy cat gave birth to as soon as possible after birth—sometimes leaving her with one. Mummy cat would cry and search for her kittens, and I would follow her and try to comfort her. I could see the milk dripping from her swollen teats. There were times when she would attempt to hide her kittens in the rows of pineapples, and if they survived they became wild and difficult for me to befriend. During my nursing career, not only did this wounding cause me to feel compassion for those who were grieving; it enabled me to understand the love a child could feel for a parent figure. There was the lesson of forgiveness to be learned. Like my parents I parented with the knowledge I had at the time. We learn what we live.

> Whatever it was that happened to you, it is over. It happened
> in the past; in the present, it does not exist unless you bring
> it with you. Nothing anyone has ever done to you has
> permanent effects, unless you hold on to it permanently.

—Marianne Williamson

While still a young child, I had another dream in which I saw a large aeroplane come over the mountain and land in a field of green beans that were waiting to be picked. Perhaps it was sent to me symbolically to transport me to a life beyond the farm and to a world of adventure? From being a child who walked several miles to a one-teacher school, and often in bare feet, I have travelled to many parts of the world and today have a sense of the oneness of all that is living. I can grasp the concept that there is one consciousness which many call God. The one's consciousness is made up of an infinite number of cells, and I see that my individual consciousness is one of those cells. With that thought, I am part of God.

I particularly relate to the need to feel a balance in my energy field. While appreciating the nurturing, guidance, and creativity I receive from the divine feminine energy, I also need the strength, courage, and adventurous energy of the divine masculine. In this memoir, I share some of what life has taught me as a nurse, mother, grandmother, and soul. It will perhaps become obvious that my little soul, strengthened by unseen hands, had a purpose to serve others in a way that was meaningful to those "others."

In a recent interview by Women's Village TV for YouTube, I was asked what advice I would give nurses who wished to follow a career in end-of-life care. I replied that they needed to be in charge of their practices. I would also add that they needed to be in charge of themselves—"know thyself" is the old adage on the ancient Greek temple in Delphi. End-of-life care is a dance between the person who is dying and the person who is offering the support. It is a sacred relationship and, in my view, fails in its duty of care if the care is not flexible and creative. I have been aware that I cannot give away what I do not have myself. If I am not peaceful in contemplating my own death, I will not be peaceful at the bedside of a dying person. We can accompany people in their life questing only as far as we ourselves have travelled, and made sense of, our own soul's journey.

My financial circumstances following the end of a thirty-year marriage supported my adventure in beginning a private nurse practice. I became the owner of several commercial buildings which gave me the financial freedom to follow my passion. At boarding school, I had been put into the commercial stream of education, and this, which seemed odd at the time, was indeed a blessing. I seemed to have a different kind of intelligence to those students and friends who achieved in the world of academia. And I certainly had an adventurous spirit that questioned the status quo. From mythologist Joseph Campbell's poem *The Warrior*:

> The world is perfect
> It is a mess
> We are not going to change it
> Our job is to straighten out
> Our own lives.

CHAPTER ONE

Professional and Personal Life

The development and creativity of my private nurse practice is intertwined with my personal life story. What follows is a combination of my personal journey and what I wrote in a six-book series, *A Passion for Caring*, for nurses who wished to follow my holistic practice.

After completing my nursing training at the Princess Alexandra Hospital in Brisbane, Australia, in February 1961, I travelled to Canada and worked in an orthopaedic ward in a Catholic hospital. I have no recollection of death ever occurring in what seemed to be an exciting new world.

Following my Canadian experience, I travelled to Edinburgh, Scotland, for midwifery training and experienced the joys and wonders of the birth of new life. The memory of the first birth I attended is still with me as I recall the proud young mother holding her newly delivered baby while talking to her husband on the bedside phone. I now see similarities in the experience of a "good birth" and the experience of a "good death." Both are charged with emotion and signify a life change that will not only entail long and sometimes arduous struggles, but also bring rewards.

After my time in Scotland, I hired a car and drove from Edinburgh to London with a map of the route as a companion. I overnighted somewhere along the way before making my way to Trafalgar Square, where I was to return the car before meeting an old school friend who had agreed to give me a bed. Looking back, I marvel at the adventurous spirit of this little country girl. Years later, and after my divorce, I made the journey in reverse, this time from London to Edinburgh in a hired car and with the intention of reclaiming some of my youthful sense of adventure. By that time I was in my late fifties, and it was a little more difficult to find the right road. At one stage, I found myself in the carpark of a large supermarket instead of on the highway I was seeking. This was before Google maps became a reality. Today, when I wonder at how information travels on the internet, I can appreciate the vastness of the mind of God.

In London for my first time, and after completing part one of my midwifery training, I worked for a private nursing agency, taking care of many rich and famous people as well as being at many births. During this time, I had a significant experience of death when the agency sent me to nurse a fifty-year-old woman who was dying of breast cancer. This patient was being cared for at home by her only child, a young woman in her mid-twenties—my age at the time. The experience was etched in my mind by its awfulness. I was instructed not to mention the word *cancer* and to express hope for recovery and confidence in the doctor. We did not name or monitor medications; we just administered them in blind faith because they had been prescribed by the doctor. The tension I experienced of keeping up this pretence and not knowing what to say to comfort the daughter and mother, who were being parted by death, was great.

When the mother died, the daughter suffered the loss profoundly. Her mother had not been allowed to help her with practical instructions for a future without her. My heart went out to this girl, and I accepted her invitation to stay in the apartment with her. Not knowing anything about a normal grief reaction, I seemed to get it all wrong. When I cleaned the walls of the bathroom, she did not show appreciation; rather, she took my actions as a reflection of inadequacy on the part of her mother. My cooking was wrong; my company was sought, but my actions were resented. I left, but the memory stayed stored in my mind for many years until the death of my own mother when she was seventy-nine and I was in my early forties.

Several weeks before my mother's last Christmas, I was walking by a dress shop when I suddenly thought of her. I went into the shop to buy her a dress for Christmas. In hindsight, this was synchronicity at play. When I arrived home, she was still on my mind. As I lived in another state, I decided to phone her. No answer. I felt uneasy. I tried to phone my brother who lived in the same country town where my mother lived. No answer. I phoned her doctor, who told me that he had admitted my mother into hospital for tests as she was unable to swallow. I arranged for her to be transferred to another hospital where the tests could be completed sooner by a surgeon I knew. I organized care for my children so that I could travel to be with her.

What alerted me to her need? I was her only daughter, and I had come along late in life, after a stillbirth and two sons. My mother's first baby died. I understand it was a breech presentation, and it must have been a very painful time for her. The baby was a girl. My mother was thirty-eight years old when I was born, and she called me Joy. I was her pure joy. Perhaps because my star sign is Sagittarius, I have always been an adventurous soul. I left home for boarding school at my own request at the age of fourteen. After boarding school, I went straight into nursing and lived in the nurses' home for four years before I ventured overseas. I had been invited by friends to join them in Spain on a holiday, as I was missing the sunshine in London. In Spain, I met an Australian man and, following an exciting courtship, we married in London. My mother must have missed the daughter of her dreams, but she accepted who I was and tried to support me. Looking back, I feel I could have been more dutiful and attentive, although the boarding school habit of writing a letter home each week remained with me. Somehow, she was prepared to pay the price for my freedom.

Following surgery, my mother was diagnosed with secondaries in the liver and an unknown primary tumour. The surgeon broke the bad news gently as he held her hand and told her he was not able to fix the problem. The private hospital staff accepted the fact their patient's daughter was a nurse who wished to be involved with her mother's care. "My daughter will shower me," my mother told the nurses. When I went to the hospital to take her home, she wore the dress I had bought during that long-distance thought connection.

We both knew that time was limited. My previous experiences of death were no preparation, so I trusted intuition and was strengthened by my mother's faith in me. My mother fought all her life for a balance between active involvement in church and community, and depression. As a small child, I felt I had two mothers and often wished, with a heavy heart, that the good fairies would take my sad mother away and bring back the one who played "Over the Waves" on the organ as I went to sleep. Music and painting were large parts of my mother's life. She played the organ for the Methodist community and was proud that one of her paintings won a prize at the Brisbane Exhibition. I now know that music and art are languages of the soul.

My mother struggled with manic depression, which forced me to be independent and self-reliant. At an early age, I learned to use the treadle Singer sewing machine to make my own underwear. I, too, was to have difficulty with my first pregnancy. My eldest son was born in London. I suffered from toxaemia and, in order to give birth to a live baby, I was given a general anaesthesia and a forceps delivery under a general anaesthesia. This caused distressed for both me and my baby. I refer to the event as my first near-death experience. Being a mother gave me much more appreciation for my mother.

When my mother came home from hospital, she chose to sleep in the front room of her small, cream-coloured brick house. This house had been built with a ramp to the back door as a homecoming for my father, who had become a quadriplegic several years before. My father died in the local small-town hospital, so his homecoming never became a reality. The front room had been kept for visitors, but now it was where my mother chose to end her days. Her garden was her pride and joy, and she knew all the botanical names of the plants in her care. The day we arrived home, her gardener came, and she could hear the reassuring sound of the lawnmower. I picked flowers from her garden and placed them in her room. The atmosphere was becoming a sacred and peaceful space. She was home. Neighbours called, and well-wishers phoned to receive the news that jaundice was setting in, and it was just a matter of time.

The local doctor made house visits and was supportive of my wish to keep her at home—at least until she became unconscious. The Uniting Church minister visited and read familiar Bible passages to her. Perhaps her biggest comfort was her little tape recorder and the Scottish tapes of empowering songs and hymns, which she played especially in the early hours of the morning when she felt most vulnerable to negative thoughts. One night she completely lost her composure and was bemoaning her worthlessness. I begged her to stay strong so I would have happy memories of our last days together. She said she was trying.

Now I say to dying parents that they are about to give their children a most precious gift, the gift of example and courage. Stories are told about the need for children to release their parents, and "letting go" is encouraged. "I'll see you tomorrow, Mum," may mean Mum will be there because that is what will please her daughter. "Mum, I know that you are having a struggle, and although I love you and will miss you, please let go if you are ready." These words are an example of how to let go in an embrace of love. So often I have said, "Love is letting go."

My mother and I had only a week together, but each moment was special as I sorted through her belongings, knowing that the time I could spend away from my four children was limited. She told me who was to have her paintings, her dinner set, the electronic organ she took to old folks' homes for sing-alongs, and her clothes. The nursing homes she visited were for other people and, although she was nearly eighty, she had never thought of being in one herself. While sorting through her desk, I came across a letter to Santa that one of my brothers had written, and I found letters of utter despair written by my mother when she had lost her connection with her God. I filled many garbage bags with what I thought was rubbish, and I put aside the special requests. I chuckled to find that she had kept her old set of dentures! I now know that haste in these matters is not a good idea, and I now regret so much having thrown out the sheet music which she had kept from her youth—including my favourite, "Over the Waves." One brother chided me for having thrown out clothes and linen which would have been useful for working on the trucks in his transport business. It was a time of high emotion and not a time for making rational decisions. My childhood memories, good and bad, were flooding over me.

My relationship with my elderly parents, my father's death—which I discovered later in my life to be a matter of unresolved grief—my rebellion against the religion of my parents, and the relationships within my own family were all issues which were surfacing. Through all this were the demands of hosting the visitors, nursing my mother, involving my two brothers in the decision making, providing food, and being concerned with the activities of my own family. I was short of sleep, and I hired a nurse so that I could spend a day with my family who had arrived at our local seaside house for a holiday.

Before I left, I organized and documented my mother's medications and opioid injections. I knew nothing in those days about hospice or the principles of palliative care, but I knew that I didn't want my mother to suffer. She was worried about her bowels—which to her mind, had to open daily—and I even organized those before I left. I gave her my word that I would return in twenty-four hours. When I did, I was greeted with a most unhappy mother who asked me why I had taken so long. The night nurse had not kept up my mother's regular injections for pain because, in her opinion, it was too early! *Too early* were words that would ring in my ears years later when I heard similar fears of morphine being expressed. How can it be too early to be comfortable when one has a terminal illness? How can it be too early for the relief of physical discomforts which hopefully will make way for regaining control of the mind and providing a pathway for connecting with the spiritual world?

From that moment, my mother's condition deteriorated. I could scarcely move her feet to get her back to bed from the commode chair. The district nurses came to help, putting my mother on an alternating pressure mattress and inserting a catheter in order to avoid the strain and stress of going to the toilet. The doctor asked if I wanted her moved to hospital. To my mother's way of thinking, nursing homes and hospitals were places to visit *other* people, and I remembered the many months of hospitals visits she had made to my father before he died. There was no way I was going to agree to move her from the security of her own bed in her own home and all that was familiar to her, no way could I abandon her to the care of strangers. There would be no more bad experiences with hired nurses. She was my mother, and I was determined to see it through. My elder brother came to support me, and we were both with her when her breathing stopped. The district nurses had just been to wash her and sit her up on her pillows. A few minutes after the realization that my mother had died sank in, the nurses appeared again. Something had told them to come back, that I needed them. A neighbour appeared and took my brother and me for a cup of tea while the nurses contacted the funeral directors and arranged for the transfer of her body. I felt as if we were all in God's guiding hands. When I returned, the bed was empty and the bedspread had been neatly replaced on the bed. It was as if the event of a few hours earlier had been erased. It was then that numbness set in.

Like a robot, I made phone calls and looked forward to lots of rest and the comfort of my own family. Later I would learn about normal grief reactions. Much later, when I began to learn about hospice care, a lot of what I experienced at this time made sense. What I did know was that I had somehow been there when I was needed—as if I had fulfilled a bargain that we had made when I was given, without guilt, my freedom to go to boarding school and to travel all those years ago. In hindsight, I realize that survival then took over and that the demands of a young family largely put my grief on hold. I took comfort from the number of people who came to the funeral service and from the letters and cards that I received and diligently answered.

For many years, moments of sadness would surface at random. They came on the golf course, they came when I received flowers, they came at my children's end-of-year school activities, they came when I wanted to share something special. The feeling I had through all my adventures was that my mother was always there—I was just like a baby playing peek-a-boo—and that while other people cared for me, no one cared in the same way. A mother's death is tied up with our own sense of beginning and ending, our own sense of love and nurture, our own sense of sacrifice and lifetime commitment. A mother's death for me was also a reminder of our ancestors and the karmic imprints we carry from their lives. These imprints derive from many lifetimes. It seems the soul's journey is never done.

From an energy perspective, a mother's love is clearly realized as an aspect of the divine feminine archetypical energy. I was a mother of four children and had a strong spirit of independence and survival, yet it was humbling, painful, and very inspirational to play a part in supporting my mother at the time of her death. It wasn't at all like the death I had experienced as a student nurse, or like the death in London of that other mother who had a daughter my age. It was an honest occasion, and I wished that more people could have this intimate knowledge of death. Energy is creative, and if I choose to allow it, the divine will influence what I create in a lifetime. Being out of alignment with divine will is what some people call "sin." Another possible definition of sin is a refusal to become conscious of our divine nature. Mystical principles are to be found in the hearts of all religions and ancient sacred scriptures. They are, in their essence, the truth.

Many years later, and following my divorce at the age of fifty-four, I had a significant dream. I was buying a ticket to enter a large concert hall. When I attempted to join the other people who were lining up to buy a ticket, I was told to go straight in as my mother had paid the price. At that time, I was very much on a spiritual quest. It was a time when contemporary mystic and author Caroline Myss was making visits to Australia as was Jean Houston, who is a world-renowned scholar, philosopher, and leader in human capacities. I was also studying Buddhism and Taoism. One of the Buddhist teachings that has stayed with me from that time is that pain and suffering come with attachment.

On reflection, I realized that my purpose during my presence as a nurse at the bedside was to encourage detachment. The German Dominican mystic Meister Eckhart (c. 1260–c. 1328) preached, "God is not found in the soul by adding anything, but by a process of subtraction." This is another way of thinking about the concept of detachment. The following quote was wisely said by Lao Tzu, the father of Taoism. "If you are depressed you are living in the past, if you are anxious you are living in the future, and if you are at peace you are living in the present." There were times when, in the role of a palliative care nurse, I talked about the collective unconscious as described by

Swiss psychiatrist, Carl G. Jung, and likened a soul to a drop of water rejoining the ocean.

I felt guided in the support I gave to patients and their families. Guided, too, to be a mentor as well as coordinator of the caring team. I would like my legacy to be that fear of death is replaced with a love of life and an energetic connection with a vast—and beyond imagination— field of consciousness. "The heart of consciousness," said neuroscientist Christof Koch, "is that it feels like something. How is it that a piece of matter, like my brain, can feel anything?" From Sufi mysticism, I was introduced to the Sufi teaching of the "hidden treasure." I (one consciousness) was a hidden treasure, so I created the world so that I might know myself and be known.

My heart has become capable of every form: It is a pasture for gazelles
    and a monastery for Christian monks, and pilgrims' Ka'ba and the
    tablets of the Torah, and the book of the Koran. I follow the religion
    of love; whatever way love's camel takes, that is my religion, my faith.

—Ibn Arabi, Sufi Mystic

As a nurse, there were times when I found my car going in a certain direction and not one that I had intended. A thought would come to me that I should check on a patient who lived in the direction my car was taking me only to find that I was, indeed, needed. On one occasion, I ignored promptings regarding a visit to an elderly patient who had been admitted to hospital and found, when I did go, that she had died. I felt regret. On this occasion, there was another lesson to be learned. While I stood at the nurses' station, an elderly woman came up to me as said: "Will you tell the nurses to let me sugar my own tea?" How many times have I done something for a patient because it was quicker?

After my mother's death, it was to be some years before my relentless restlessness prodded me to return to nursing. I had not practised my profession for twenty years, and fortunately, a shortage of nurses meant the opportunity to complete a refresher course at a large teaching hospital came my way. It was difficult to step out of my routine of children's activities, working part time in my husband's orthodontic practice, playing bridge and golf, giving dinner parties, and going on exciting holidays to enter a world of regular working hours, two-thousand-word essays, and wearing the blue uniform of a refresher student. During this time of study, death was to, again, confront me in an unpleasant way. I observed that even the doctors and nurses had a fear of death and a way of distancing themselves from death. This fear was frequently masked behind hospital procedures and rituals which replaced a genuine concern for the real needs of the person or individual soul.

On one memorable day, I observed that one of the patients in the ward was near death from cancer. The disease had progressed and was blocking the flow of lymph from the woman's leg. The leg needed to be supported on a pillow, and every movement was agony for this elderly woman who appeared to have no family support. One of the nurses on duty chose to withhold her morphine medication because, in her assessment, it lowered the patient's blood pressure too much. I was bewildered at this priority, and my heart went out to the woman who was clearly suffering. I expressed my concern for this nurse's action in the best way I could. Thankfully, in a more enlightened way, the hospice movement has the intention to put the patient's comfort first through providing good palliative care. In this discipline of medicine, relieving pain and managing physical and other discomforts are of paramount importance. Palliative care nursing became a passion for me for three decades. I not only nursed people who were nearing the end of their lives, but also elderly people who chose to be supported in their homes.

CHAPTER TWO

Influences on My Models of Care

I was the founding director of Private Palliative Care Services, Pty Ltd, which traded as NurseLink and was launched in 1987. My goal was to offer private, personal, and flexible care supervised by nurses in the home environment. Sometimes care was given in the person's own home and sometimes it complemented the care given in an aged care facility. My models have been a work in progress. I was a foundation executive member of NIPPSA (Nurses in Private Practice, South Australia) and have encouraged and supported nurses in their business aspirations to take their place alongside other allied health professionals such as speech therapists, physiotherapists, dieticians, and others. The focus of my practice was gerontology and palliative care. While I was the principal nurse consultant, I employed other nurses and palliative care assistants on a casual basis. I also employed office personnel as time went on and the practice grew. It was a team approach. Ongoing education and personal development were cornerstones.

Soon after my practice was launched, I had the opportunity to attend a life, death, and transition workshop organized by the Elisabeth Kübler-Ross Association and held in the Adelaide Hills. At this workshop, a booklet titled "The Dougy Letter—A Letter to a Dying Child," written by Dr. Elisabeth Kübler-Ross was circulated. Dougy was a nine-year-old boy who was dying from cancer. In the Letter to Dougy, there were three circular diagrams, each circle divided into four quadrants. The first diagram depicted the seasons and stated that everything in life is a circle: day follows night, spring comes after winter. On the second circle, which depicted day and night, there was a sailing ship on the circumference of the circle with these words: "When a boat disappears behind the horizon, it is not 'gone,' just out of our sight. God watches over everything that He created—the earth, the sun, trees, flowers and people—who have to get through the school of life before they graduate." The third diagram was labelled "Man," and the four quadrants were named: Intellectual (Thinking), (Physical Body), Emotional (Feelings) and Spiritual (God). This diagram inspired me to use the model of four quadrants as a basis for my holistic nursing care.

The core of my model and a guide to holistic care:

Spiritual

Searching:

- for meaning in life and self
- for personal values and beliefs
- for trusting relationships

Practising:

- meditation, contemplation, and prayer
- living in present moment with love
- listening to and trusting intuition
- appreciation of nature and the natural order

Physical

Obtaining:

- relief from troublesome symptoms
- appropriate nutrition
- bowel and bladder care

Experiencing:

- comfort and safety
- therapeutic touch and massage
- frequent hygiene
- periods of rest and activity

Emotional

Experiencing:

- unconditional love
- forgiveness of self and others
- choice

Feeling:

- a sense of freedom and control
- the comfort of belonging
- a sense of usefulness and satisfaction and role
- the peace of being in the present moment

Intellectual

Obtaining:

- health information
- involvement in decision making
- effective communication

Understanding:

- benefits of positive approaches
- changes need not promote stress
- legal aspects of living
- funeral planning

The core of this practice model demonstrates ways to support a person's multi-layered needs and to make practical not only a person's physical and intellectual needs, but also his or her emotional and spiritual needs. It acknowledges that all these areas are interrelated and need equal attention. Of equal importance in the concept of holistic health is the interrelatedness of body, mind, soul, and spirit. If a patient was having difficulty with constipation, I might ask him or her about other things they were holding onto and perhaps needed to release. Food is so much more than nutrition. It is memories of a mother's cooking, a wedding feast, a time of poverty or other deprecation, or even the symbolic bread and wine of communion in a religious ceremony. I have known patients who avoided certain foods because of unhappy connections and others who craved foods that were connected with life celebrations. I have experienced a release of emotion during a massage I was having, and I have witnessed similar releases when giving a massage to patients in my care. It seems that muscles store memories, and this contributes to muscle tension. The emotion of anxiety is frequently felt in the body and may be felt as sweaty palms or butterflies in the stomach. Many patients had a fear of dying or a God-related fear that impacted on their sleep and rest. Emotional and spiritual discomforts may have defied explanation in the intellect. We don't know what we don't know. So much of us exists in the unconscious.

Following the life, death, and transition workshop and a visit to a nurses' healers' conference in New York State in the United States, I developed a particular interest in the interrelatedness of body, mind, spirit, and soul. To gain an understanding of my own personality as well as studying personality types, I studied the Enneagram. However, it was the work of Swiss psychologist Carl G. Jung and the symbolic concepts of the conscious, the unconscious, and collective unconscious aspects of the self, which Jung described as the total timeless man, that spoke to me the most. The self, from my understanding of Jung's work, is much more than the ego, which differentiates one person from another and is the work of the first half of life. The second half of life is concerned with soul searching and is driven by the larger self, or soul, to find meaning and purpose. A crisis is not uncommon in midlife when these changes are occurring. I know that my restlessness began in midlife. At this time, I was becoming more soul driven. I was searching for larger aspects of life, and I began to gain insights from metaphors and myths. I felt in agreement with, and inspired by, the work of humanist psychologist Abraham Maslow of Maslow's hierarchy of needs fame and Erik Erikson for his theory on the psychosocial development of human beings in his eight stages of man.

People who are faced with life-threatening illnesses and who are in search of meaning may choose to respond to their illnesses as some sort of mythical wounding which has the potential to alter the course of their lives. I frequently heard the phrase "a person breaks down to break through." The catalyst for change may have been a cancer diagnosis, the loss of a job, loss through another's death, or some other "little death" such as losing one's physical appearance or status in the world. In order to view these little deaths or losses in a different light and with a soul's journey in mind, I began to study wide ranging areas of my own personal development and healing. I became qualified as a Myers-Briggs Typology consultant and obtained a post graduate certificate in bereavement and palliative care counselling from the Department of Medicine at Adelaide University. I learned to have an appreciation of complementary therapies and became an accredited practitioner of therapeutic touch, Reiki, and neuro-linguistic programing. In 2013, I obtained a diploma in clinical hypnosis. Self-directed learning was my approach then and is still so today, although today I can take advantage of the internet for webinars and courses.

As I write, I am a student in a webinar course with Thomas Huble, a contemporary global spiritual teacher. I am learning how trauma of this lifetime and past lifetimes can impact the way we die—how there is a need to integrate the past and present with the future. As a young man, Thomas studied medicine for six years before finding his vocation as a teacher of mystical principles. His teaching is about growing and flowing while in alignment with the soul's purpose. It is about bringing to light the darkness or shadows of our lives and healing those hidden parts. It is about realizing that the influence of collective trauma such as war atrocities and the pain inflicted on women lives on in the unconscious. End of life is a time for understanding higher consciousness in a way that acknowledges that each person will be in a different grade in the school of life. While we all make progress at different levels of understanding or consciousness, we are all connected and feel the pain others are experiencing.

For me, becoming more conscious of the wisdom to be found in thousands of years of tradition has been a step-by-step process. I found this wise saying to be true: "When the student is ready, the teacher appears." In the beginning of my re-entry into the healthcare system I was introduced to Ian Gawler's work. He was a veterinarian who had cured himself of osteosarcoma (a type of bone cancer) with secondary spread. He became a prominent advocate for the therapeutic application of mind-body medicine and meditation. I knew his oncologist, who lived in my city. He encouraged me to attend the education that was provided by the Cancer Care Centre in Adelaide. This community-based organization provides complementary care services in the support of people affected by cancer. I also became familiar with the work of Dr. O. Carl Simonton, a US radiation oncologist who popularized the mind-body connection in fighting cancer with techniques such as meditation and imagery. What appealed to me was the fact that he gave patients a sense of control over their illness and encouraged a therapeutic partnership in care. I became more and more conscious of the fact that people receiving care knew much more about their lives and their bodies than I or any health professional could possibly know. Hippocrates, the father of modern medicine, in 500 BC, said that it is more important to know the person than it is to know the disease.

Early on, I attended a workshop given by John Harrison, a doctor who had written a book titled *Love Your Disease: It is Keeping You Healthy.* This book helped me develop an appreciation of the complexity of the lives we lead and that it is a common feeling that illness and hardship should be rewarded in some way. Yes, I came across people who controlled family members by using emotional ties. The ill person may have unconsciously observed, *Why get better when I can command this attention?* It seemed that, if positive strokes were not being obtained, then negative ones would be sought. I came across people who were dying who needed to separate from close family members so that they could concentrate on getting to know the needs of their own bodies and souls. They needed space from emotional and physical attachment. This was the case for a young mother of two children who was dying of cancer. She sent her husband to live separately for a time while she concentrated on staying well. Her parents were very involved in looking after the children and supporting her as much as they could. She died at home, and her husband and children were with her when she took her last breath. That was the time I witnessed a valuable lesson. The husband lifted their two small children onto the bed and showed them that mummy wasn't breathing anymore. He suggested that they take off mummy's rings, which would always remind them of her. For me this was such a far cry from a medical approach to care, and it seemed so natural.

Care and support are all about the patient, and they need to agree with the goals set by clinicians. If this is so, the outcome from this "partnership in care" will be more predictable. When I was doing my refresher course at a large teaching hospital, one student wrote a poem about "pushing the pen"—writing everything down—being more important than hands-on patient care. In some cases, nursing care was documented but not necessarily done. The drive for accreditation to obtain government or other funding meant that looking good on paper seemed to be more valued than actual actions carried out. Hopefully the pendulum is swinging back to an appreciation of the intangible elements of caring. A more enlightened way is to provide holistic patient-centred care and appreciate that all life is a spark of the universal energy. We are souls having a physical experience. Pierre Teilhard de Chardin, who was a famous French philosopher and a Jesuit priest, puts it this way: "We are not human beings having a spiritual experience. We are spiritual beings having a human experience." On mind-body medicine, one oncologist put it this way: "The intravenous infusion of chemotherapy is likely to be more effective if the patient thinks positively and imagines it is a healing stream of medication rather than referring to it as their regular dose of poison." This was my early introduction to caring in a person-centred, mind-body, and holistic way.

After I had run my practice for seven years, my husband told me that he didn't want to support my "dying business" anymore and that it would be better if we were to separate. It was a difficult time. We were both Catholics and regular church attendees, and we both included our children in this lifestyle. The era of the Second Vatican Council had brought many welcome changes, if not lifting the ban on contraception. After my refresher course, I worked at the Mary Potter Hospice, which was founded by The Little Company of Mary. In this environment, I was introduced to women who had become nuns of various orders. I sometimes referred to myself as a "secular nun," knowing that a vow of obedience in the real world of nuns would not sit lightly on my progressive "boss" archetype. Before returning to nursing, I had worked part time in my husband's orthodontic office and had introduced an early computer system for accounting. I fell in love with computers, and during my refresher course, I used a word processor for my care plans and notes. My creative right-sided brain was very active during my time at Mary Potter Hospice, and while not everyone was keen to make changes and grow, Sister Ignatius, the hospital administrator, suggested that a hospice foundation would perhaps provide some of the equipment I was suggesting would improve the comfort of those in care. Together we organized the launch of the Mary Potter Foundation. Today this organization is going from strength to strength.

During that time, I was deeply questioning my faith in the religion I had adopted at my marriage. Even in high school, and before I became a Catholic, I loved to read poems by English poet and Jesuit priest, Gerard Manley Hopkins. When I was questioning my faith, I decided that it is better to save a soul than to save a marriage. My soul seemed to be on an unstoppable journey. Kahlil Gibran, the Lebanese poet and philosopher, in his book, *The Prophet,* wrote this on marriage: "Love one another, but make not a bond of love; let it rather be a moving sea between the shores of your souls." The changes in the Catholic Church's teachings were giving a soul much more freedom in the way it lived and served God, and I welcomed the fact that I no longer had to eat fish on a Friday. I found connectedness in Sophia, a spirituality centre that had been built by a Dominican order of nuns. One nun in particular was to guide me. Margaret Cain was the visionary who introduced me to the Enneagram and Jungian concepts. For me her saying, "Life has meaning when we give ourselves meaning," became a basis for the educational courses I ran through my practice. Through the ups and downs of my life as a nurse—and there were many times when I wanted to end the responsibilities I had taken on—I looked for the lesson I was meant to learn.

All my experiences were leading me to encourage more personal responsibility—in myself and others. I travelled to a therapeutic touch conference in California after my divorce and met another nun who befriended me. She offered to drive me to the mother house of her order in San Francisco and to give me accommodation for several nights. This was my introduction to the meditative music of the Taizé Community, a monastic order founded in France by Brother Rogers as an ecumenical brotherhood. Today, this community is made up of over a hundred brothers, including Catholics and brothers from various Protestant backgrounds from around thirty nations. I had several cassettes of Taizé music, which I offered to patients who were seeking a meditative approach as death neared.

Developing a "therapeutic relationship" in care rather than depending on the professional "knowing best" and having complete control was gradually becoming a way of care introduced to me by Dr. Carl Simonton; Dr. Ian Gawler; emeritus professor of palliative care Ian Maddocks, AM; and others in the health setting. I was impressed by the fact that Ian Maddocks, who was the first professor of palliative care in the world, humbly gave his mobile phone number to his patients. I followed suit. I welcomed progressive nuns as friends and began to see the difference between a religious life and a spiritual life. One of these nun friends said that the mind is like a parachute and functions best when fully open! I plan to write more about their influence in a future book, and I intend to write about issues such as euthanasia and reincarnation.

A man I went to visit in my role as hospice nurse was to greatly influence my career and demonstrate the power of the mind when combined with a faith in God. (Remember that God has many names.)

I was told to visit this man to tell him about the services the hospice offered. He jokingly tells me today when I see him that he was my first hospice patient in 1987, and in 2017 he is still alive! I apparently said all the wrong things on that first visit, and he was not at all interested in hearing about the hospice. His cancer had begun on his lower lip and had spread to his neck and lungs. He had undergone extensive surgery, but his will to live and his faith in God greatly influenced the outcome of the surgery. He was left with a quarter of a lung and many scars. He refused to have chemotherapy after questioning the percentages of its success. His wife juiced carrots and natural herbs and gave him hands-on healing. I visited him following the lung surgery and suggested that a physiotherapist might be able to show him some helpful breathing exercises. He refused, but he accepted an invitation to have a game of golf with me. At the end of the day, with a twinkle in his eye, he boasted that his score was better than mine! He went on to work for an overseas Christian mission, flying to foreign countries despite his reduced lung capacity and generally taking charge of his life. There seemed to be nothing he could not do if he set his mind to it. He was to make my first promotional video.

Making videos was an interest he established after he sold his farm. As I look back on our relationship, I see him as a guardian angel who was sent to help me. I had spent nearly all my savings on a promotional video, stationery, rented office space, and a business launch. Not only did referrals not come my way, but a large government hospital threatened to sue me for using one of their patients in my video. The woman was a friend of my video maker and was being cared for in her own home at the time we made the video. When does a hospital own a patient? This was daunting for a nurse who was just spreading her wings. I was grateful to have a lawyer friend for support, and eventually the matter was resolved with letters to and from the hospital board. Another early struggle was obtaining a rebate for my nursing services from the private health insurers. One such insurer did support me in this way for many years. In reality, it was the work of the palliative care assistants that needed a rebate. So my way of care was truly a market-driven, fee-for-service model.

I have often described myself as being a midwife to the dying. One Irish man and his wife came to see me in my office to ask about care at home when the time came. He was full of the Irish blarney, and there was much light heartedness in the interview. I didn't hear from him again for many months, and I feared that I may not have conducted the interview in a serious enough manner—we both seemed to have enjoyed the interaction. However, just like the phrase "call the midwife" applies to the impending birth of a baby, a similar phrase applied to the impending death of this man. His wife phoned me. "He said, 'It's time for Joy.'" I spent several weeks visiting them prior to his death to make sure everyone was "on the same page"—an expression I used frequently. Then, in the early hours of one morning, I received a call to say that he had needed to go to the bathroom and couldn't be moved. When I arrived, an ambulance and the police were there. If a person dies at home, the ambulance attendants are required to call for the police to attend. In this case, they helped me get the man's body onto a bed so that I could wash and dress him. I returned in the morning to find that his wife, who suffered from dementia, had forgotten that her husband had died. Fortunately, their daughter was in charge. She was able to offer comfort to her mother, and she decided on the clothes to send to the funeral people. This is an example of death being a family affair rather than a hospital affair.

CHAPTER THREE

My Time in Malaysia

At the time of my divorce, I was president of Women Chiefs of Enterprises International (WCEI) for my state. I had only ever experienced family holidays and, finding myself living alone, I was inspired to attend a WCEI conference in Malaysia as a way of following an interest and having a break. With business in mind, I read of a fundraising walk for the Malaysian Hospice Association and contacted the secretary, Elisabeth Alfred. We connected immediately when she told me that she had completed her nursing education in my home city. She said that what was needed in Malaysia at that time was palliative care or hospice education. I had found that I needed those who wished to work for me to be educated in the hospice philosophy and innovative ways of providing medication for pain relief and symptom management as well as considering psycho-social needs. The newly appointed professor of palliative care at the Flinders University in Adelaide was Ian Maddocks. Along with a Malaysian-born nurse-educator from Flinders University, this remarkable man graciously accepted my invitation to assist me in presenting the first formal palliative care education in Malaysia, in Kuala Lumpur. It was attended by over a hundred doctors and nurses and was to introduce me to a role in palliative care education in West and East Malaysia that would last for more than a decade. At this time, I had been awarded the academic status of associate lecturer (Level A) in the School of Nursing, Faculty of Health Sciences, at Flinders University of South Australia.

The first invitation I received to work in West Malaysia came from a Chinese oncologist working in Kuala Lumpur and Ipoh. Living by faith, I agreed to spend three months in Ipoh assisting in the establishment of a private hospice and giving talks on palliative care. At the time, I was a Rotarian and was made very welcome by the local Rotary Club in Ipoh. I was very impressed with Rotary in Malaysia and noted that there were more women members than in my club back home. During this time, I attended a large Rotary gathering in Kuala Lumpur and was proud of the young Australians representing their country. They respectfully wore ties and were formally dressed, as was the local custom. I was included in many Rotary activities in Ipoh. One I particularly remember was an Indian wedding complete with all the cultural customs. The local people were very friendly towards this Australian nurse who was to give many lectures on the topic of palliative care as defined by the World Health Organization. I could not speak the language, and the food, climate, and culture were unfamiliar to me—an adventure. I learned, in the Indian way, to eat with my fingers from food served on a banana leaf and to use chopsticks for the many delicious Chinese meals I experienced. I became accustomed to eating chilli, bitter melon, pomelo (a citrus fruit), durian (a fruit that smells terrible), and many other exotic fruits. It was surprising to see two Methodist churches close to each other for different races to worship. Yet, there was harmony and respect for differences. I formed strong friendships, which continue to this day.

Prior to going to Malaysia, I had two significant dreams. In one I was riding in an elevator when the projection suddenly took off at a right angle as if it was taking me overseas. In another I was playing golf, and my ball landed in a bunker. The bunker contained water, and my ball had disappeared into it. The bunker was close to the green, and I could clearly see the flagstick marking the hole. Yet, when I connected with the submerged ball, it went in an entirely different and unexpected direction. In waking life, this is just what did happen. I was to have shown to me the difference between promises, expectations, and experience. My vision of how to create a new life for myself and to spread the benefits of a palliative approach to end of life was to swing to a different fairway rather than to the one I anticipated in Ipoh. It appeared that the setting up of a private hospice in Ipoh was fraught with more challenges than could be met. I became disentangled from a difficult situation that was beyond my control. I lost money but gained strength of character and a small understanding of another way of life that was not predominately British, which was the origin of my ancestors.

For the three months that I lived in Malaysia I learned much about the running of "old folks" homes. And, perhaps, years later, my work there had a small influence in the setting up of an excellent establishment for the care of the elderly in Ipoh by the Yayasan Lotus Foundation. My talks on complementary therapies were always well received, and there was an interest in emotional and spiritual pain. While I was in Malaysia, I was invited by other government organizations to give talks on palliative care. A government car and Indian driver were provided. I felt very inadequate having only English as my language. Hopefully, my overhead slides conveyed a little of what my spoken word could not. One day I had a meal in an Indian restaurant with the driver. When the food was presented on a banana leaf, the driver thoughtfully requested a fork for my use. One of these sessions was being held at the Klang Hospital. I was pleased to learn that this hospital had been designed by my mentor, Florence Nightingale. In the years that followed, I was to learn much more about her contribution to the wider world than just her contribution in the Crimean War. The people I met were immensely kind, and one nurse from Klang looked into registering my NurseLink Company in Malaysia. This required me to have a Malaysian partner. I also went through the process of registering as a nurse in Malaysia. To do this, I needed to be employed by someone rather than self-employed. Many of my creative ideas were thwarted by red tape and reliance on known ways of doing things.

While I was in Ipoh, I attended a palliative care conference in Penang to give a paper on a research project on palliative care models. With three other male academic nurses, NurseLink had received a grant from the commonwealth government prior to my going to Malaysia. The aim of the project was to define the diversity and effectiveness of existing palliative care models in rural and urban settings. Primary models included institutionally based hospice care, care focused on keeping people in their own homes, and community-based nursing home care. My private palliative care model, NurseLink, was an adjunctive model and was described as a case-coordination model providing hospice at home. It was stated that, in this model, limited infrastructure is needed, and the primary carers are usually nurses. While patients and carers reported the benefits of dying at home because of freedom and flexibility, it was the large, government-funded organizations that employed many people working as a multidisciplinary team that dominated the report. The report was finalized in 1997.

From my point of view, it was a case of David and Goliath. I talked about the primary nurse being multi-skilled in end-of life-care—like a doctor in general practice. She or he would seek other services only on a needs basis, and with the permission of the patient. My argument was that patients in the private sector didn't wish to have a multidisciplinary team to relate to at this sensitive time of their lives. They wished to remain in charge and live life their way. They wanted to die in character privately, and with as little fuss as possible. These patients did not see themselves as cases to be discussed in a team meeting at which they had no direct say. My role, as well as being case coordinator, was to be an advocate for these patients. In spite of letters to my local minister of health explaining my model and how it had the potential to change the way end-of-life care was delivered and the advantages of expanding the role for the nurse, no support was forthcoming. One politician told me, rather cynically, that the government doesn't support excellence! However, twenty years later I was still practising my model of care and being appreciated by those in my care and those I employed.

It seemed difficult for some to value the work of a nurse, especially one that was self-employed. I was not good at marketing my brand of care and felt uncomfortable with hyperbole. I was comforted by hearing an end-of-year speech given at the private school my sons attended. The presenter was a governor of the state. He said that, if you are not being criticized, you are not doing anything worthwhile. Criticized I was. If I asked a question at a palliative care meeting, it was likely to be met with an audience member rolling his or her eyes. This was the case when

I questioned a man who was talking about his mother's death and the needs of the family. I asked him if his mother believed in a life after death. In my experience, a person's belief concerning life after death influences how the person who is dying reaches a peaceful state. For some, this is a private matter, I was told, and I sensed a divide between what doctors and nurses provide by way of palliative care and what is outsourced to chaplains. My way was to be more holistic.

From the international meeting in Penang, where I nervously gave an overview of the research I had initiated, I was invited to give a talk to the hospital staff in Seremban, Malaysia. It was appreciated that I was self-funding my time in Malaysia, and the matron of the hospital kindly offered me hospitality in her home. I will never forget her kindness or the turtle ornaments she gave me. I was later to learn that the turtle is my totem animal in the Shamanic tradition. It was in Seremban that I made contact with another Rotarian, and the idea of a matching grant between two districts in Malaysia and my local Rotary Club was conceived. The matching grant was for a month's education on palliative care for doctors and nurses from Malaysia to be held in Adelaide. I came home and began work on obtaining a matching grant from Rotary International, two district clubs in Malaysia, and my local club. It was an enormous amount of work, but it was deemed by all who participated to have been a worthwhile project.

Twenty-four doctors, nurses, and volunteers from Malaysia came to Adelaide for a month to study our world-class palliative care facilities. Flinders University of South Australia pioneered palliative education under the guidance of Professor Ian Maddocks. With this program, our knowledge was being shared with our neighbours. I met the group at the airport in my traditional Malaysian costume, known as *baju kurung*. In typical Malaysian style, a large banner was produced for a group photograph. A welcome was hosted by the Royal Adelaide Hospital where they were housed in the former nurses' quarters. Each weekday morning, a bus would arrive to take the group to the place of study and observation. I accompanied our friends from Malaysia each day. At weekends, they were hosted by other Rotary clubs for barbecues and even a trip on our Murray River. There were many photo opportunities as they visited many sites, including pain clinics, hospices, district nursing services, and nursing homes. We had several days at NurseLink, and following their return, I was invited to go to East Malaysia by a most progressive nurse, Margaret Lieu, to conduct the first volunteer training for their community hospice. This educational support for their hospice program continued for a period of ten years. I was honoured to have Professor Ian Maddock and Professor David Currow share their knowledge and wisdom at these sessions. I have such fond memories of these visits, and they have given me an appreciation of Eastern philosophies and cultures.

In 1999, I was proud to accept a certificate of membership from the World Wide Network of Women of Vision and Action. This is a network of women who believe in applying qualities of vision, compassion, courage, and spirit-based action in daily life and in the fulfilment of their life's mission. Malaysia is a Muslim country, and the women I met owned businesses and held positions of management in hospitals and universities. On several occasions, I was invited to their homes. One kind lady offered to make clothes for me in the Malaysian style. She talked freely of her beliefs and way of life. On another occasion, I enjoyed being invited to a night for women where clothes, linens, and head scarves were being offered for sale. On my return to Australia, I found myself disputing a commonly held view of the life of Muslim women as being repressed and unhappily restricted. I also visited Chinese and Muslim homes where there were multiple wives. I was impressed to see a younger wife looking after the children and caring for an older wife who was dying.

When I reflect on my time in Malaysia, where I experienced different religious and marriage customs, I am reminded of the mystical principle that we are all one. In 2015, on a guided tour of Southern India with Andrew Harvey, I visited the ashram (a place of spiritual retreat) of Ramana Maharshi. While I was meditating in the room where this saint listened to those seeking his wisdom, I had a profound vision. I saw myself clearly, and in colour, dipping my toe in a clear flowing stream, which I felt was a stream of consciousness. Then the visual image changed, and I saw myself opening the slot in a door by pouring smooth, rich, yellow custard into it from a pewter jug. This image I still find puzzling. Perhaps it is a message to open doors with flowing and comforting food—food for the soul as a way of opening the door to the next world? I still remember the saint's bright eyes, which seemed to follow me around the ashram. I feel my time in Malaysia introduced me to new ways of accepting divine guidance.

Obviously, I could not just leave my practice in Adelaide when I agreed to go to Malaysia, and many arrangements needed to be put in place. I had employed nurses and office staff to care for the nursing practice, which was beginning an accreditation process. In retrospect, I realize that I was in a state of grief over leaving a thirty-year marriage and dealing with all the implications for a single life and for relationships with my four young-adult children who were making their own way in the world. Whatever the reason, I may have unwittingly given these staff members the impression that I was abandoning them in some way. When I did return from Malaysia, I discovered that the nurses and the carer coordinator had set up their own private businesses—one for nurses and one for carers. In reality, I needed to begin the process of building a caring team all over again. This time I did so with a franchise model in mind. This meant producing policies and procedures in great detail. With the help of a lawyer and my accountant, I put a toe in the water of franchising. My ambition was for nurses to set up their own practices with my support and experience. The computer software that had been especially written would be part of the franchise package.

It was a very idealist ambition. The concept was that the nurses would pay a token fee for the documents, website, advertising, and computer program, and the company I set up would take a percentage of their gross earnings. This way, if they were not earning, they did not have to pay fees. One nurse in another state, whose husband was a lawyer, did buy a franchise. Training was completed in Adelaide, and support through phone and email communication was frequent. This nurse experienced, as I also did, that support was lacking from other nurses and the traditional service providers. Another factor was that it was difficult to recruit and maintain casual staff to be the arms and legs of the practice nurse. This nurse found that her patients wanted her exclusively. This made it difficult to grow the business. Practice income relied on hours spent with the patient, and the goal was something like four hundred hours of caring per week by the caring team. Looking after elderly patients in their own homes provided the main practice income. Care and support for palliative care patients was intense, and my way of care also had an addictive quality. There is a saying in end-of-life care that patients need not fear becoming addictive to morphine (or other medication) to keep them comfortable; rather, carers who work in this field should the fear of addiction to their work. Many of my caring team loved the work to the point of addiction, and almost all referrals for patients and carers came by word of mouth.

I finally abandoned the model. The timing was just not right. Additionally, there was a lack of adequate financial backing, and I had to consider the needs of my own family. With regard to family needs I had a choice. I could assist financially my family's interest in establishing the Bird in Hand winery, or I could employ personnel to advance the franchise I had envisioned. When it came to superannuation, I also chose to direct capital into the winery rather than security for my old age. This was intuitive guidance that is supporting me today.

However, before I abandoned the idea of the franchise, I was to be honoured with the prestigious award of Social Entrepreneur of the Year for the Central Region of Australia in 2007. Ernst & Young, a multinational company which, in Adelaide, provides accounting and auditing services, began the Entrepreneur of the Year program in Australia in 2001. The aim of this program is to recognize the most successful and innovative entrepreneurs in various categories of endeavour. While I did not win the National award, it was a thrill to represent my region and to mingle with the other contestants and our mentors from Ernst & Young (known as EY today). It was also a thrill to have an opportunity to tell my story! My motto was recorded as: "Give and don't count the cost." This is true. The goal of financial gain was never my motivation. It was all about doing what I love, and felt called, to do.

In the program's magazine for that year, my significant personal achievement was recorded as engaging in wide-ranging personal and professional development—seeking to understand meaning and purpose in life. My major business achievement was listed as providing a cost-effective model of care with the nurse as the coordinator of a caring team. The caring team not only received employment, but also gained a measure of self-esteem. Many of the team members I trained were people who received a pension or simply wished to make a contribution to society in some way. They were not all working for the goal of making money. "Givers fare far better than takers when it comes to having a meaningful life" are words from Caroline Myss. When asked how I recharge personally, I said that I use the sea, swimming, travelling, warm weather, and cooking to recharge and get ready for the next challenges that present themselves. Today, I would say walking in nature and the spiritual practice of going within with mantra and meditation!

CHAPTER FOUR

Developing Attitude, Knowledge, and Skills

During my working life, I attended work-related conferences in Canada, the US, the UK, Thailand, Singapore, India, and Malaysia. In 2001, I travelled to Chiang Mai University in Thailand to give a presentation on "Palliative Care: Integrating Science and Spirituality" at the International Conference, "Improving Life through Health Promotion: Nurses Making a Difference." The nursing profession in Thailand has a long history of receiving royal patronage because one of their queens had been a nurse. My visit to Chiang Mai was also memorable because it happened just before I had eye surgery for cataracts. As a visitor to Thailand, I was taken to visit a silk manufacturing business. I purchased a length of silk, which I thought was a delicate mushroom pink. Following surgery, I was surprised to discover that the silk was indeed a very bright pink colour! From these travels and my keenness to maintain a broad knowledge base, I have gained insights into the interwoven threads of values and beliefs that are common to all people.

Early on I was introduced to *The Tibetan Way of Dying*, a book written by Sogal Rinpoche and edited by Patrick Gaffney and Andrew Harvey. It became my guide and inspiration. In 2015, I met Andrew Harvey on a study tour of Southern India. This meeting seemed to be by synchronicity, as part of the time I spent with Andrew was in the ashram where Bede Griffith spent his last days. Bede Griffiths' book,

The Marriage of East and West, was given to me in 1994 by the nurse in charge of St. Leonard's Hospice in England. A visit to this site was part of an international hospice and palliative care study seminar in the UK. I remember being amazed at the wisdom contained in that book. Bede Griffiths, who was a British-born Benedictine monk and priest, wrote that there is a craving for warmth, for closeness, and for intimacy in every human being.

As a business and professional woman, I worked in my former husband's orthodontic practice and became enthusiastic about using computers for a range of administrative activities and record-keeping. My attitude to life is that I am here to learn and to embrace the new technologies and to use them in service to others. I was the CEO of NurseLink Foundation, which was launched in 2006 to further the work of my nurse practice and end-of-life education. I was an associate fellow of the Australian Institute of Management, South Australian president of Women Chiefs of Enterprises International, co-founder of the Mary Potter Foundation, a Rotarian, and a member of many professional organizations. Before I began my practice, I completed two subjects, accounting and finance, and management information systems, at the School of Business, University of South Australia. In writing this book I have attempted to encapsulate my insights from a long nursing career into a practical holistic care model for any nurse who seeks to follow in my footsteps.

I needed to have more than qualifications. My greatest challenge was to understand the unconscious part of a person—how it affected not only my life, but also the lives of others. There are several ways to tap into the unconscious: meditation, mindfulness, and by observing the feelings that we see and feel mirrored in another person. Our songs, movies, and dreams are examples of idealistic romantic love and desires. We look for a template of our desires in another. We are driven and influenced by our relationships. Relationships include a relationship with one's self, with others, and with the eternal one creative force. Jack Kornfield, who is a teacher in American Theravada Buddhism, writes that the other person becomes the ideal that awakens our own loving hearts. We may transfer onto the other person our longings, so he or she carries beauty, strength, courage, and intelligence—all qualities that we may possess without knowing it. The effectiveness of transferring, rather than owning, admired qualities in ourselves may be short lived if the other person doesn't live up to our expectations. This can most commonly be seen in a marriage partnership.

Before I went to Malaysia, I had begun the process of writing policies and procedures. Perhaps in my less-self-aware way, I was wanting the criticism and blame that was sometimes levelled at me personally by those I employed to rest with the policies and procedures. That way the policy and procedures could be the target rather than Joy, and as they were inanimate, they could be more easily changed. With the wisdom of hindsight, I now realize that I was probably not in a healthy space in my life.

Looking back on my practice years, I can acknowledge that dying patients have taught me so much. Firstly, they have taught me to examine my own mortality and to take time to listen to the inner world of my soul. Secondly, they have taught me about their needs—sometimes expressed clearly, and sometimes veiled in idle chatter and innuendo. Most importantly, I needed to listen openly and without trying to fix the situation. People remember you by the way you make them feel.

Some of the things my patients have said:

- Please *listen* to what I am *not* telling you.
- Help me to stay strong and calm in my beliefs.
- Help me to be proud of the way I am facing a life-threatening illness.
- Help me with my fears, which include my "dark night" of doubt and disbelief.
- Let me die *my* way rather than *your* way.
- Let me have a say in where I die.
- Help me and/or my family with preparing my funeral.
- Help me to embrace insecurity and detachment.
- Make my body comfortable so that I can concentrate on my mind.

- Let *me* evaluate the effect of the medications for pain and troublesome symptoms.
- Help my family when I have gone.
- Be still, unhurried, and gentle
- Be consistent and work as a team—leave behind personal jealousies and problems.
- Let me go on fighting if that is my nature.
- Let me be resigned to my fate and refuse treatment if that is my wish.
- Help me to find some worth in my life.
- Let me feel loved without conditions.
- Let me feel forgiven and forgiving.
- Give me information so that I can make choices.
- Respect the emotions that well up from the depths of my soul, for they inform my unmet needs.
- Help me to put in place significant mementos for family and friends.
- Facilitate people from my religion if I request a visit.
- Be patient when I change my mind and seem unappreciative.
- Realize that sounds such as music, birds, and the sea and symbols such as flowers and religious objects can comfort more than words.
- Let me withdraw, be sad, or even cry.

I believe what is needed is an attitude that says "I'm here to give love and care for you, with agreed conditions, and without needing gratitude." Caring for the dying is a privilege, and those who do so need to reflect an attitude that removes fear and gives confidence and reassurance. Nurses need to be aware of the need to resolve their own past losses and feel secure and peaceful within themselves. Often potential palliative care assistants asked me what qualifications were required to work for me. I always answered that the first qualification was to be a good person with a kind and caring heart capable of giving love and compassion. When it came to patient care, I would assess the needs of all involved and brief the carers in ways to fulfil those needs without negating the patient's own sense of self. Direct and indirect supervision was given during what could be seen as on-the-job training. A cost-effective way of care needed to be maintained, as there was no government funding. I was pleased when my practice became a part of NurseLink Foundation, which was a not-for-profit charity launched in 2006.

Intention is the key word: "I intend to be supportive in a positive and patient-centred way." I recall being taken to see a woman in her home in Malaysia. She had breast cancer, and I was introduced to her by the local hospice team. I could not speak her language, and she could not speak mine. My heart went out to her, and my intention was to offer comfort with a smile and caring hands. The daughter who had flown in from Switzerland observed and asked if I was giving her mother Reiki. I was amazed that, here we were from many parts of the world, yet we were connected with the giving of healing energy and intention in action. Perhaps we are too accustomed to the belief that disease and death are tragic, and we miss the beauty of simple interactions. I cringe when I hear that a person "lost his or her battle with cancer." Fighting has such negative connotations, and it is connected to feelings of anger and right and wrong. Olivia Newton-John, AO, OBE who is an English-Australian singer, songwriter, and actress, also avoids the word *battle* and prefers to say that her cancer is lovingly being carried away. We are accustomed to believe that disease and death are tragic when they can be viewed as a reminder to change our ways. While the mind tries to fix reality into a pattern that is understood, and keeps a person safe, the pattern may come from the past and may not serve us in the present.

A nurse can develop an unhelpful attitude through unresolved grief, curiosity about death, guilt, and shame over an event in her or his own life. It is not helpful to have an attitude of knowing best that negates the patient's own sense of self and also devalues his or her known and trusted support systems. This attitude may leave a patient in a confused state rather than with feelings of empowerment. It is, after all, a personal life and soul journey. Each patient does his or her best with the knowledge he or she has at that time. When I worked in the hospice, one of the nurses persuaded an elderly person who had been living on the street with his wine-drinking mates to come into the hospice. She was proud of the fact that he died in clean sheets, but I felt that she was meeting her needs rather than those of the elderly man, who may have felt more at home with his mates and being supported in his dying with them rather than in clean sheets. Giving this man a choice would have empowered him. An empowering attitude gives informed consent and honours the person's choice. However, with choice comes responsibility, and I realize that not everyone wants to take responsibility for his or her own decisions—perhaps that is best left to karma!

Professional staff may also unintentionally impose ideas that are contrary to the patient's beliefs. These ideas may concern treatments or daily routines such as eating, drinking, and other physical needs. A "normal" routine may be to sleep at night and be awake in the daytime. I found that many people, as they neared death, experienced a reversal of day and night. It may be that they found daytime busy and distracting, while the quiet night allowed them to get in touch with their inner guide or God. A non-judgemental attitude can be difficult to maintain because we all have unconscious projections that benefit from being brought to awareness. In my book, *As Good as Goodbyes Get: A Window into Death and Dying,* I wrote about my early experiences and projecting my own unresolved grief from my father's death onto patients in the hospice. He had a bedsore when he died, and this, for me, was a nurse's disgrace. Yet, in retrospect, this realization gave me the energy to raise funds so the hospice could provide better resources.

In hospice education, those caring for the dying are encouraged to know about different cultures and so increase their knowledge of the variations—and the similarities—in spiritual care. Many people have lost association with a traditional religion, and comprehensive care needs to fill this gap. An open attitude with respect for "oneness" is essential. Giving information and sharing an appropriate part of one's own life can be helpful and build trust, especially if there is some common ground such as coming from the same parts of the country, believing in the same religion, or holding similar beliefs and values. I think about connecting with the energy of the seven main chakras as a road map. This concept leads the conversation from the personal origins of the base chakra through the activities of the sacral, solar plexus, heart, throat, third eye chakra, to the crown. These areas of energy need to be explored with great sensitivity, but such exploration has the potential to break through trivial conversation to reach a level of depth which can be described as a soul-to-soul conversation. For the most part, the safer ground is to begin the caring relationship by striving to give unconditional love and to honour the dying person for himself or herself in a non-judgemental way.

In brief, health professionals and volunteers need to have a working knowledge of the medications used to relieve pain and promote comfort. For some people, medications are accepted as a major component of the management of discomfort in end-of-life care, but they are not the only options. Other options involve information, understanding, and acceptance. In my practice, there was "on-call" support as well as emotional support for all concerned. Everyone involved had to understand the normal processes of grief and pending loss. They needed to understand the spiritual significance of death. It was helpful to know what resources are available and where to access information on a range of issues from various non-drug treatments, including complementary therapies, to providing someone to speak the dying person's language. Nurses trained in palliative care are valuable in assisting a person to make an advance care directive. They have experienced and witnessed the death experience and what can precede it. The adage "people don't know what they don't know" highlights the limitations of people who are documenting what they perceive to be in their best interest.

I have heard nurses opting out of asking questions other than those that pertain to the body. Their excuse is that the answers to those questions are private. Being comfortable in one's own skin and secure in one's own search for "the deep and meaningful" is essential for effective total care. How one obtains this awareness depends largely on internal guidance or connection with the unseen world. Even when a person is near to dying, the concept of wellness is important to maintain: a person can die "well." Consider the metaphor of the body being a person's vehicle through life. If one of the tyres receives a puncture, the "thorn" that caused the problem needs to be removed before the tyre can be mended and the journey continued in a balanced way. It may be helpful to consider the soul as the vehicle that transports a person through a lifetime.

There is so much knowledge to be obtained in order to work successfully in the area of care for the dying. Dame Cicely Saunders, the founder of the modern hospice movement, wrote that hospice is about bringing to the bedside the best science has to offer along with the best of the heart. I remember hearing her speak at St. Christopher's Hospice in London. She spoke of total pain and how the physical pain of a man in the hospice was compounded by the pain he felt for his wife who had to catch two buses to visit him. While good intentions and scientific knowledge are important, there is so much more to supporting a person at the end of life. There needs to be knowledge of the self, or soul, as well as the different parts that make up the personality. Esoteric philosophy describes self as a physical body, an emotional body, and a mental body. Different religious traditions offer wisdom that transcends thoughts that are doggedly considered to be true. I appreciated studying humanistic psychology and the work of Abraham Maslow and Carl Rogers on self-actualization, self-worth, and positive regard, as well as cognitive behavioural therapy.

There are many courses being offered at different levels on the origins of the hospice philosophy, legal and ethical considerations, principles and goals of treatment, psychological and spiritual concerns, and counselling strategies, all of which are essential. Knowledge of one's own stress levels and finding ways of dealing with that stress are vital in self-care and the continuing care of another person. Eckhart Tolle, who is the author of *The Power of Now: A Guide to Spiritual Enlightenment,* says that stress is being in conflict with the "now" or "what is." Tolle describes this state as an intensely alive state that is free of time, free of problems, free of thinking, free of the burden of the personality. Living in this state is a spiritual practice which requires giving space to yourself and to others. He also recommends paying attention to the space or gap between words, for that enables the light of consciousness to shine through. I see death as a spiritual event rather than a medical event. In 2017, I attended one of Eckhart Tolle's Australian weekend retreats where he spoke of the "now" as the experience of a surfer pausing and being "in the moment" on the crest of a wave. His philosophy is that difficulties are given to us to help us to awaken.

My life has certainly taken me out of my comfort zone. At one point in my life, I had a vitreous haemorrhage in my right eye. I could see thin streaks of black moving down my eye. Eye surgery followed to remove the haemorrhage, and more surgeries followed to prevent my retina from collapsing. Today I have impaired vision in that eye, and I was left with surgically induced glaucoma. My mantra in difficult times has been "The strong sword goes through fire." To be able to listen to the heartache and loss embedded in another's story, I found it helpful to search for and give an example of a "silver lining." I like to give examples of how other people chose to handle a particular experience. *Reframing* is a counselling term. What is important is that the new thinking about a situation comes from the person's own insight. The ego, or sense of "I-ness," looks for comfort. However, spiritual awakening often comes from the difficult times. There are times when life events and physical ailments take people out of their comfort zones. I needed to acknowledge these times in my own life and see them as opportunities for personal growth. Before my eye surgery, I spent a week for health professionals at the Ian Gawler Retreat Centre. I needed to change the way I responded to what life was giving me rather than becoming a victim. This way of accepting illness or injury could perhaps enhance the traditional medical palliative care model. Life surely challenges.

We take ourselves to our work, and it is difficult to mop up another's tears if we are a "wet towel" ourselves. I have said that, if I cannot look after myself, I cannot look after another. I am here to learn and to become conscious.

There are many psychological tools used in business and institutions to promote self-knowledge. The Myers-Briggs Typology is one such tool that I have found useful. It evolved from the work of Swiss psychiatrist Carl Jung. I appreciate his model of the conscious self, the unconscious self, and the collective unconscious where we are all connected. Another term Jung used was "the shadow." The shadow is that part of the unconscious that contains life events which have been suppressed, and desires and wishes not realized. Many spiritual teachers refer to the shadow. Carl Jung said, "Unless you learn to face your own shadows, you will continue to see them in others, because the world outside you is only a reflection of the world inside you." I agree with Jung's statement that, in the second part of a person's life, a person is driven by spiritual drives rather than ego needs. Spiritual drives include becoming familiar with one's shadow.

There are times when real problems may arise in a person's unconscious and are revealed by projection onto another person. An understanding of this is helpful for those who are caring for the dying so that they realize that many problems and expressions of anger arise from unconscious issues, and that strong emotions which may be expressed are just that—a release. Feelings are not rational or right or wrong. They need safe expression rather than projection onto another person. Emotions differ from feelings. Emotions tend to be felt in the body, whereas feelings are felt in the mind. Emotions may be apparent as a nervous tummy, trouble breathing, sweaty palms, trembling legs, tears, headache, nausea, backache, muscles spasms, smiles, and frowns. Feelings are recognized in the mind. We experience feelings of anxiety, nervousness, grief, shame, stress, fear, guilt, empathy, being stuck, frustration, tenseness, overwhelm, sadness, happiness, and bewilderment. However, the mind may be so busy telling feelings what they should be that a person might fail to let feelings be recognized for what they actually are. Naomi Feil, validation therapist, wrote, "Freud, Jung, and Erikson have documented that denied emotions grow, locked inside, and give physical pain."

From Eckhart Tolle in his book, *A New Earth: Awakening to Your Life's Purpose,* I learned to appreciate the energy field called "ego" and also the collection of emotional energy which he calls the "pain body." These energy fields are mostly unconscious, and it takes considerable insight to become aware of the influences they wield in our lives and in the health of our physical bodies. So many of us suppress aspects of our lives which cause us to be distressed. This distress Elisabeth Kübler-Ross described as a "pocket of pus" that needs to be released so that the healing can take place. What is in the unconscious is seen in symptoms and irritations and what we like and do not like in another person or object. This is why a holistic approach or integrated approach to healthcare is always necessary. There may not be time for professional psychotherapy, but much can be achieved with visualizations for releasing what is not useful or does not serve our well-being. Hypnosis is also a very useful therapy for releasing what is buried in the unconscious. The conscious mind is always aware of what happens during hypnosis.

Perhaps the most important skill of all is the ability to simply be a non-judgemental friend. For this to happen, it is essential to build a trusting relationship. One of my elderly patients once called me at four o'clock one morning and told me that she had spilt a glass of water in her bed. While I was travelling to her home to repair the damage, I felt that what was really happening was a trial of trust. For a patient to have the courage to cease futile treatment, take medicine aimed at promoting comfort, and mentally prepare to detach from this life, trust in the caring team and a healthy actualized sense of self is required. Remember the power of praise and that little things matter. I always tried to remember how patients liked to have their cups of tea and what names they preferred to be called. Not everyone likes to be called by his or her first name, and most patients actively dislike being called "dear" or "pop."

Hospitals have become such strong symbols of places where people go to receive lifesaving surgery and treatment so they can get better. Hospice is a new symbol that removes fear and promotes comfort, empowerment, and reassurance. The Mary Potter Hospice Foundation was co-founded by Sister Ignatius and myself. Sister Ignatius was a nun with the Little Company of Mary. This Catholic order's founder was a nun, Mary Potter, and she taught that the dying needed to be cared for with a mother's love. This is a profound statement and one that is seldom incorporated into a clinical pathway. I view it this way: I aimed to psychologically transfer onto those in my care the empathetic feelings—which include love—that I imagine Mary felt as she stood at the foot of the cross on which her son was nailed.

It is also important to look at the whole person and not just an aspect of a recently learned theory. On one occasion, I was to mentor a new palliative care assistant who had recently acquired a certificate in aged care. She was to spend her first night with a woman who was nearing her hundredth birthday. This woman spoke twelve languages, had travelled extensively, and had run an antique business in two countries. In the morning, I phoned the new recruit to inquire about the night. She told me in glowing terms that she had cooked an evening meal for the patient and advised her that she had too much butter in her diet! I could imagine how that would annoy a woman of her age and experience who was entirely happy to take responsibility for her own life. My view was that we needed to respect her choice of eating butter and empower her in ways that rather nourished her soul.

The most effective skill I know is to be yourself and in the present moment of eternal *now*, as Eckhart Tolle expresses it. Another way is to practise listening to the gap between words. Communication is a skill, and it occurs on many levels. The body has a language as does a person's energy field. There is power in a smile as well as in a gentle touch. A valuable skill is to be an effective advocate for the patient and family. There is also the skill of exchanging positive energy and so removing fear and changing a person's moodiness. When a person is feeling "light," his or her energy may be said to be positive; conversely, when a person is feeling "heavy," his or her energy is said to be negative. Fear and depression are heavy feelings which may be lifted or diluted by the presence of a person who is feeling "light and lovely."

It takes skill to recognize symptoms in the emotional body and the mental body as well as in the physical body. This is the role of energy medicine. Above all, there is the skill for communicating in a spiritual language that is appropriate to the person's spiritual needs. I have stated many times that I am an agnostic Buddhist Catholic and a person who loves to recite Buddhist and Sufi mantras. My concept of a mantra is that it steadies my mind and keeps negative thoughts from intruding on a peaceful state. When I practice a mantra, I am making the spiritual more familiar— like taking a familiar road home in my car. I relate to Sogyal Rimpoche, the Tibetan Buddhist master, when he says that he believes in the nature of God but not the concept of God. Music, art, and poetry are all languages the soul uses to heighten awareness of energy that arises from within.

All health professionals and institutions need to work hand in hand in a non-competitive way to promote patient-centred care. It may be difficult for some health professionals to take off the professional mask or approach, but to my mind nursing a person who is dying is about having empathy and being prepared to let go of the need to be right or to know what is best. The patient first—always!

CHAPTER FIVE

Love and Compassion in Action

Many writers describe the various stages a person goes through after receiving a life-threatening diagnosis. The Swiss psychiatrist Elisabeth Kübler-Ross, who has written so much about death and dying, describes stages of anger, denial, bargaining, depression, and acceptance. An attitude which may be helpful to some is one that honours a supreme being: "Thy will be done, not my will." An attitude of detachment from ego and the trappings of the material world may help to promote a sense of "letting go," acceptance, and a calm mind. Bringing a patient to an attitude of forgiveness both of self and of others may also assist in bringing peace. It is difficult to build a trusting relationship based on deceit and lies, and many families believe that their attitude of keeping up appearances and not telling the patient of the seriousness of his or her illness is in the patient's best interests. This may not be so for those patients who wish to consciously prepare for their impending death. The appropriate attitude in breaking bad news is a sensitive issue, and there is no one right answer; every situation requires an individual approach.

The amount of information given to the "unit of care" (the patient, family members, and friends) depends on many factors; however, information given regarding choices may assist in facilitating actions directed at promoting quality of life—a term frequently used in hospice work. Choices may include considering the advantage of ceasing treatment aimed at cure where previous case studies show there to be little or no benefit from that treatment. Categories of medication, including vitamin supplements, may be another choice. Some patients may wish to rely on techniques that involve using the mind rather than using medications. Others may wish to know about complementary therapies such as Reiki, massage, and essences from plants and flowers. Some patients may choose to die at home while others will find comfort and security while being cared for in a special building such as an aged care facility, hospice, or palliative care unit in a hospital.

I liked to give the people in my care the choice of a celebratory drink at a posh hotel or a final swim in the sea. One strong-minded lady expressed the need to attend a church to receive a final communion. With great effort, I managed to get her to the church; however, before communion, I glanced at her pale face and decided to get her back to my car, which was parked near a side door. I went back inside and found a priest who volunteered to take communion to her in my car. We were not leaving without receiving the sacred host! We joked about having "drive-in communion." Returning to her Catholic faith had been a recent event for her, and I willingly assisted in her request. The thought occurred to me that it would not have been a bad thing if she had died in the church. Could a loving church community have seen this woman's death in a holy place to be a gift? Death all too often is seen as something to be avoided and feared. She died a week later, and her small funeral service was held in the same church. I recognize the value in being a doer, but I also know the value of just being quietly present. Simple things do make a difference.

Even when I worked in the hospice, I would see eyebrows raise when I offered to facilitate a final game of bridge for a woman who had loved her game of bridge. In those days, I was still playing golf, and I told one man in a hospice bed that I had him in my mind when I scored well. That brought happiness to his hollow eyes. I usually worked in my nursing role at weekends when the atmosphere seemed to be more relaxed. One day I offered to give a man a shave and a haircut. With assistance, I got him positioned in a chair beside his bed and draped a draw sheet around his shoulders. When I lived in Rochester, New York, with my husband while he was studying orthodontics, we were poor. We saved money when I cut his hair. Now here I was cutting a patient's hair. After the shave and haircut, I said: "Well, we have the physical side looking good—what about the legal side of things?" This man's sister was sitting by the bed watching the procedure and immediately opened her bag to produce a standard will document. She hadn't known how to bring up the need for it to be completed. Love and laughter flowed.

While at the hospice I was challenged to find ways that were acceptable to use my feminine energy as part of my caring. Every day seemed to be the same. The thought occurred to me that the days could be differentiated by putting a different flower on the meal tray for each day. If it was a rose, it must be Monday. One man whom I had known in the community came into the hospice but decried the fact that there was nothing to do except to watch the hands on the clock next to his bed. Even in his weakened state, and with the help of oxygen delivered by long tubing, he could visit his shed at home. Some choose to "burn out rather than rust out" as they face end of life. Elisabeth Kübler-Ross taught that people die in character. It is difficult to satisfy individual needs in an institutional setting. Whose needs are we meeting? I know that I am a risk taker and do not wish to be wrapped in hip protectors and kept behind bedrails for my safety. As a private nurse, I would visit a man who was in a nursing home and record his memoir on my laptop. Following a session, we would share a glass of sherry, which he kept in his cupboard—what fun! Yes, I did flirt a little with my patients. I saw it as an exchange of happy energy.

The skills of communication are essential to patient-centred care. I needed to learn how powerful our words can be and to avoid being misunderstood. In today's world, many find comfort in being able to communicate with emails and texts. I found that men particularly chose this type of communication as it was less emotionally confronting than face-to-face sharing. I would often suggest a walk on the beach as part of a bereavement follow-up. There were times when the patient and the family members refrained from asking questions for fear of sounding ignorant or foolish. Intuition was a valued guide in determining the real issue—as well as welcoming criticism as merely feedback. There are different levels of communication, and there were times when I knew not to "go there"—at least not at that time. Just as a broken limb needs a cast for support until it heals, so too a person may need the protection of denial until the time is right to heal a painful emotion.

At an educational session in Malaysia on communication, I asked participants to work in pairs and to discuss different levels of communication until they were able to ask the "big question"—is there life after death? I observed one pair—a man and a woman—smiling broadly. When I asked them the reason, the man replied that he was a Muslim and his fellow course participant was a Christian, and yet they both believed in heaven! There was joy in the air following this simple, yet deep, exchange.

Dame Cicely Saunders referred to the family as a "unit of care." A member of this unit may well wish to develop nursing skills with guidance from those who are trained in various areas of healthcare. This may include dressing wounds, monitoring medications, taking care of the skin, promoting comforting hygiene, and providing nourishing food and restful periods. Settling a sick person for the night is a skill. At a nurse healers' conference in New York, I listened to a nurse suggest the use of trance in settling a patient for the night. This is the example she gave of a nurse giving a patient her night time medication: "Mrs. Smith, I have your medication. It will give you a good night's sleep." In contrast, less effective words might be: "Mrs. Smith, I have your medication. It *might* help you sleep." Of course, the tone of the voice and a smiling caring face all contribute to the trance suggestion. I would also suggest sprinkling some lavender essential oil on the pillow.

Sensitivity is required when suggesting the need for adaptations to be made to the home environment for safety concerns. There may be a need to replace furniture, remove mats, and improve lighting to compensate for failing strength. My role as case coordinator was to determine what the self-care failings were and to offer support that would keep the person receiving care in control as much as possible. This was his or her end of life, and my goals were to empower the person, as well as provide confidence in a realistic way. I acknowledge that my attitude to the care I gave was influenced by what I had learned and observed from my time as a young nurse caring in the private sector in London. Sensitivity to another's needs was called for when a patient who was nearly blind requested her carer place her toiletries back exactly as she had found them rather than tidy them away. When taking a history of dietary needs, in the home situation, I would document the name of the food and the way it was to be served rather than the type of diet that should be followed. The same applied to drinks, whether it was alcohol or tea and coffee. These small thoughtful acts saved repeated questioning and were appreciated.

Perhaps I inherited my lifelong love of flowers from my mother. On my sixtieth birthday, I invited family members and friends to a celebration dinner at a beautiful heritage house, now a restaurant, in Adelaide. I requested no presents other than credit for flowers with the florist next door to my practice. That way I could have flowers for a whole year. I loved being able to pop in for a special order of flowers. There were times when I would order a single bloom to take with me when I visited a patient in hospital. Many times, I would receive flowers by way of a "thank you," and my heart would swell. When my book, *As Good as Goodbyes Get—A Window into Death and Dying*, was launched in New York City in 2015, I received a beautiful bouquet of flowers from my mentors, Jean Houston and Peggy Rubin. This made the occasion an even more special one. Yes, there were friends and celebrities at the launch lunch, which my youngest son organized—yet the flowers conveyed much.

I believe the following quote encapsulates the hospice philosophy.

The Bridge

There are times in life when we are called to be bridges,
not a great monument spanning a distance and carrying
loads of heavy traffic, but a simple bridge to help one
person from here to there over some difficulty—such as
pain, grief, fear, loneliness, a bridge which opens the
way for ongoing journey …

—Joy Cowley

Soygal Rinpoche, the Tibetan Buddhist teacher who has inspired people in the Western world, said that there would be no chance to get to know death at all if it happened only once. Every change has the potential to bring loss and feelings of grief. The death of dreams, desires, and the things we cling to may be seen as "practice" deaths for the death of the physical body. I found that there were people who, having lost faith in a former religion, would be comforted with descriptions of the dying process that stemmed from the Buddhist philosophy of "dying by the four elements"–earth, water, fire, and air. For example, the element of earth could be appreciated as a "'sinking into the earth" feeling when the body became weak. With this element, eyesight blurs and a lack of blood circulation can be seen in the body as extremities become blue and cold. One patient, who was a doctor, calmly drew my attention to the fact that his peripheral circulation was diminishing.

The water element is experienced when the body fluids dry up—urine, mucus, and saliva. Reduced urine was usually collected via a catheter and drainage bag hidden in the bed. This had the advantage of containing any odour and the need to move the patient when all looked peaceful. It also gave those in the vigil uninterrupted time at the bedside. I would use an alternating air mattress to protect the skin at this time. A tray of products used for oral hygiene would be close by. This is a time for excellence in oral hygiene and keeping the mouth and lips moist. There were times when relatives would ask about giving intravenous fluids. I would explain that I understood the kidneys and other organs to be shutting down in the normal process of dying and that such fluids might delay the natural process. Having said that, there were times when the natural process of dying was delayed for an important event such a child needing to say goodbye. Who decides? What can people live with? These are questions without ready answers and require much contemplation. The World Health Organization guidelines state that palliative care neither hastens nor postpones death.

The element of fire can be felt when the temperature of the body increases (although the extremities remain cold) as if the energy of the person is gathering in the chakra channels ready for departure. This is a time to adjust the bedclothes and room temperature. I would explain that it was a normal part of dying, and medication was not required to reduce the temperature in the body. Caroline Myss wrote that, according to energy medicine, we are all living history books. Our bodies contain our history—every chapter, line, and verse of every event and relationship in our lives. I like to imagine these history particles being carried on the energy that leaves the body via the chakra channels. The crown chakra is the most favoured portal for this energy as it leaves the body. I have yet much to learn about a person's different energy bodies.

One day one of my sons asked if I could bring a Buddhist monk to give his newborn son a blessing. On the car journey, I asked the monk why I placed such importance on making sure a patient's hair was shampooed clean and encouraged people at the bedside to bring their attention to the top of the head with soothing strokes and gentle tapping. This seemed to me to be what my intuition was telling me, as I knew little about chakras at that time in my life. The monk replied that I must have brought into this lifetime a karmic imprint of this knowledge. I seemed to know when it was time to move from giving the feet and legs a massage to giving attention to the heart chakra and to the crown chakra. My intention, it seemed, was to move from keeping the energy earthbound to encouraging it to leave the body.

The final stage of air is seen with the sign of irregular breathing and the wind finally taking the breath away. I would observe these changes without trying to alter them. One woman who was unafraid of death asked me if her throat irritations were the "death rattles." I replied: "No, not yet!" In the early days of working in a hospice there were many times when I observed that the giving of oxygen prolonged the person's dying. When the person became unconscious, this treatment seemed to be prolonging death rather than prolonging life. I have also encountered very elderly patients whom I thought would be more comfortable having oxygen to relieve their breathing when it became laboured during morning hygiene, only to have the doctor refuse to order it.

After the death of a patient, I placed great importance on the ritual of bathing and dressing the body that had become lifeless. As one woman said to me: "He is still my husband even if he is not breathing." I would be there, when possible, for the transfer of the body to the funeral people. Ritual was also important for the transfer, and there were times when a guard of honour was formed from the person's home to the waiting vehicle which would transfer the body to the funeral home. A flower of two was sometimes picked from the garden to be placed on the form of the body, now covered respectfully. One grieving widow placed her husband's hat where others had placed flowers. It was a lived and open experience—rather than one being outsourced to others. Family members were invited to help me wash and dress the body following death, and for many this was a profound healing and helpful experience. When I first worked in the hospice, it was customary to use special linen on the bed following the bathing and dressing of the body. The bedspread and matching pillowcases were elaborate. A lighted candle (today an electric version) was placed on the bedside table, and chairs were placed near the bed for that final hand holding and goodbye. I continued the habit of respecting these rituals.

I learned that, in a trusting relationship, a person lying beside the patient in a bed could be as comforting, or more comforting, than medication. I always encouraged this action. There were times, in the middle of the night, when the human warmth provided by an embrace was all that we had to offer. One man who was discharged from hospital to die at home had been placed in a hospital bed to make the providing of nursing care a bit easier. He and his recently married wife had been lovers in their early lives but had been separated by life events. Now they were expected by health professionals to spend their new-found togetherness in separate rooms. No way! With help from strong friends, the dying man was lifted on a sheet into a double bed where his wife could join him. I remember kneeling beside the bed and stroking his head as I took him through a visualization of time spent in central Australia. His wife was beside him in their love bed. That was the way he died.

Much of my practice was caring for people who were dying because of age rather than disease. Keeping people at home as long as possible, even if that means taking some risks, prolongs that sense of self. Dementia in all its forms is a terminal illness, and supporting a person with dementia is difficult. I would advise my carers to avoid asking questions and to just talk feelings. The greatest difficulty I encountered was the fact that impaired cognitive ability prevents reason, and often those with dementia have no clear understanding of their needs or of the concerns felt by those close to them. There are times when their repetitive movements replace words, and they express past conflicts in a disguised form such as accusations of stealing. Above all, they needed to feel that someone loved them. The comfort that a pet can bring is not to be underestimated. I have observed cats and dogs behave in ways that indicated the change in a person's energy field.

In one case, there was a complaint from a daughter that her mother didn't change her dress frequently enough. This elderly woman would become very upset when the morning carer offered her a different dress to the one hanging on the wardrobe door from the night before. At some level of consciousness, the dress hanging on the door from the day before gave her a sense of where she was, and who she was. No amount of explanation could calm the situation. We learned, however, that we could exchange the dress for a fresh one after she had fallen asleep. The ritual of hanging the dress on the door—rather than the dress itself—provided security. There was a need to see her actions through her eyes. Love is present in many situations—from cooking a meal to appreciating the workmanship in a piece of furniture. Like many of my patients, I felt the presence of love in many an antique piece of furniture or portrait. Another subtle energy is commonly sensed when a person cooks a favourite meal that cannot even be eaten. I would remind people that the loving intention is the real "'food."

When a person with dementia is moved into an institution, all the familiar rituals are lost along with the other household prompts that afforded a measure of recognition and security. This is sad, but sometimes necessary. Some families appreciated this fact and paid for nursing at home care. In their minds, it was their parents' money and they wanted it spent on them. Other families comforted themselves that nursing homes provided the best professional care. There are many factors to consider in dementia cases. Sometimes my carers would be asked to visit the patient with dementia in the aged care facility so that a known face could offer some reassurance. The soul decides when it is time to die, but it is often silenced with words like these: "I'm not ready to let my mother go yet." "Pain and suffering come with attachment" are words that come to my mind in these situations. The energy of the mother archetype is powerful, and when the form of the birth mother is threatened, there is the choice to evoke support from another archetype—survivor, independent child, Mother Nature, or Divine Mother.

I viewed dementia as a terminal illness and offered a palliative care approach to the person's daily living. That meant serving food which afforded good memories rather than maintaining good nutrition as the main goal. It meant consulting with the doctor and family about medications that could be ceased if they were not intended to make the body and mind comfortable. It meant providing exercise in a natural garden setting rather than in a formal physiotherapy setting. It meant feeding the birds, stoking an animal, arranging flowers, revisiting greeting cards and photographs that had been saved. I would respect a refusal to eat or drink. Sadly, some people cannot voice discomforting symptoms; therefore, it is vital to observe for any signs and sounds of distress. This requires continuity of care and comprehensive documentation.

Validation therapy, as described by Naomi Feil, taught me the importance of trust when caring for an elderly disoriented person. She also taught that that their sense of identity comes from within. This may result in a characteristically very proper, polite woman with dementia showing opposite behaviour to what had been previously been expected of her. It may be seen as a kindness to a small child by a gruff seemingly cold-hearted man. Bowel and bladder management need creative strategies because a reliable answer to a question is not to be had. A damaged brain cannot control emotions such as anger, fear, love, and sorrow. Triggers for outbursts, once identified, can be avoided or allowed to dissolve in an atmosphere of trust. I would remind carers to remember the power of praise. Find some small thing to praise.

CHAPTER SIX

More about My Practice

My early struggles and ambitions are described in Chapter 6 of *Issues in Australian Nursing (3 1992)*. Elizabeth Dunsmore, member of the Academy of Management (AOM), in her role as clinical nurse consultant, palliative care, Flinders Medical Centre, South Australia, has written about the role NurseLink played in offering private palliative care services along with services offered by other palliative care programmes and the Royal District Nursing Service, in a paper presented in Vienna, August 1992. This paper formed part of an International Conference on Cancer Nursing. Her paper was titled "Politics in Palliative Care—The Nurse's Role." I presented a paper entitled "A Private Nurse Practice" at the International Images of Health—Philosophical and Political Dimensions conference held at the University of Ballarat in 1996. My goal was for NurseLink to be an example of nursing excellence and to be recognized as a pioneer in community nurse practice, and a developer and marketer of products and systems to support nurses who wished to start a community nurse practice. I wanted to be an influential promoter of nursing in order for nurse visits to be added to the list of Allied Health professionals who qualified for Medicare rebates. The valuable final product was to be an organization that progressed the art of nursing in the Florence Nightingale tradition.

I called my practice NurseLink because it represented a nurse providing a link between the patient, the patient's family members, and the health team. Experience with NurseLink confirmed that many individuals and families in the private sector appreciated patient-centred care in their own environment, surrounded by the people and the things they knew and loved. This gave them a sense of confidence and control. Other people felt more confident and secure in traditional healthcare settings with a nurse visit from NurseLink. My early motto was "The patient first—always." It later became "Supporting Life to the End."

There are many factors which influenced the place of death. For some people who were facing death, the thought that they were making it easier for the family to cope influenced the decision. Others may have had a memory of a home death that had been filled with fear. Respecting informed choice, and in some cases, dispelling fears by offering twenty-four-hour support, made a difference. Rewards for those providing the service went beyond financial payments and included gaining experience and insights into another person's way of life and the opportunity for developing compassion and personal growth. Caroline Myss wrote that "givers" fare far better than "takers" when it comes to having a meaning life.

An experienced registered nurse was responsible for the initial assessment of a prospective patient and for coordinating the ongoing care. The service provided personal and flexible twenty-four-hour care that included an on-call helpline. This meant that the patient and family members were empowered to self-care. The NurseLink team members were there to fill in any gaps in the self-care with education and practical help. Counselling went hand in hand with practical care. It is well known that important conversations are often held when the dishes are being washed. There is togetherness in an ordinary task. Giving honour to the way people have lived their lives and solved their own problems was part of the self-actualization process. Treatments and procedures were reviewed with consideration to burdens and benefits experienced. All people have the right to refuse treatment and care. Ideally, treatment and care are supportive and flexible. Feedback was encouraged, and I often found that a phone call from a family member about one topic, such as an account, was in reality a need to connect about a deeper matter that was troubling them.

This is the heart of my model of care.

Physical needs looked at the management of pain and troublesome symptoms (for example, nausea, incontinence, and constipation), meeting hygiene and nutrition needs, providing support in an environment of choice.

Intellectual needs looked at receiving information relating to health and family, and helping the patient to be involved in decision making and accepting change, attending to legal matters, and living mindfully in the present moment.

Emotional needs looked at helping the patient to experience choice and feeling purposeful, and to reflect on life and resolve "unfinished business." It also focused on helping the patient to grieve, heal, and let go. No fear!

Spiritual needs looked at helping the patient to transcend the mind and become conscious of divine formless cosmic "love energy" as he or she was guided by internal wisdom and the eternal soul.

The model recognized the multiple layers of a person's needs and strove to support not only a person's physical and intellectual needs, but also emotional and spiritual needs. It acknowledged that all these areas are interrelated and need equal attention. This requires time. For some patients, a few hours a week were sufficient; for others, twenty-four-hour care was necessary.

The NurseLink portfolio was the assessment tool. It contained health information, invited the patient and family members to explore their own needs and, with the guidance of the case coordinator, to form mutual goals. The role of the case coordinator was to put into place care that supported individual preferences with consideration being given to the costs involved in providing that care. The patient and family members were encouraged to live their lives in ways that were meaningful for them. Choice was always an option, and trusting relationships and information underpinned the choices.

The patient portfolio was central to the team and was kept in the patient's home to provide effective continuity of communication for all those involved in the care. The patient and family could read what was reported; after all, it was all about their care. This resulted in some creative ways of describing an incident. One male patient who had dementia wanted to behave inappropriately with a carer, and the incident was recorded as the patient thinking he was on his honeymoon! The case coordinator maximized the use of known resources, and the role included advocacy as well as education and counselling. Documentation encouraged each team member to consider the whole person when writing a report for the period of care. A weekly work schedule advised who was coming and the time and contract of care. This document was signed, and it became an input document for the computer system for the generation of accounts to the patient and payments to staff. The practice model provided scope and satisfaction for the nurse case coordinator. A commitment to ongoing education and self-awareness was undertaken by all members of the caring team. The induction package from the personnel procedures section was a comprehensive guide to employees and was presented as a separate document, as was the patient portfolio.

Mentoring, supervising, and credentialing all played a part in the network of care NurseLink provided for the members of the caring team as well as for those registered nurses who were encouraged to be case coordinators. Being a nurse in business as a sole trader was daunting. I was committed to quality control, and the practice was eventually accredited with an international standard. For this accreditation, we received a grant from the government. We also received GST-free status as a nursing service. To my mind, total care of a patient included looking after his or her home environment. The patient and environment are one when it comes to feeling happy and secure.

The symbolic diagram below was an attempt to illustrate the unseen parts of a person that exceeded all human experience and definition. My language was not equipped to deal with a reality such as the One God, the Cosmic Christ or Nirvana (to Buddhists the ultimate reality). I like the Taoist saying: "The Tao [God] that can be known is not the Tao." Language, which is a concept of mind, is not equipped to describe a reality beyond the mind. Each individual creates the image of God that works for him or her. Spiritual practices such as yoga and meditation have made people aware of their inner dimensions. When words are inadequate, myths and archetypes (psychological patterns) have been described by searchers for the meaning in life and in life's relationships. For example, if a woman is described as "'a good mother," we have an image and understanding of the archetype.

My Energy Model

Spirit

- Energy that gives animation
- Connecting with the God in you—a divine spark
- The divine feminine and divine masculine in action

The subtle bodies

- Physical—dense energy vibrations
- The etheric body vibrates at higher frequency—personal aura
- Emotional and mental bodies are beyond the etheric

Soul

- The immortal deepest true self which journeys over many lifetimes
- I become what is in my soul—karmic imprints
- Tunes in to the world and into spirit and returns to oneness

Mind

- Image becomes concept— to explore, to fathom, to construct, to reason
- Consciousness
- Original mind—the silence between thoughts

Janet Macrae records in the book she edited with Michael Calabria, *Suggestions for Thought by Florence Nightingale—selections and commentaries:*

> Nightingale's philosophy revolved around a Spirit of Right, a Perfect Being possessing a wise and benevolent will … She never seems to have had a morbid attitude toward death, always regarding it as an integral part of the divine plan. As a young woman of twenty-six, she wrote: "Death is the arch of triumph under which the soul passes to live again in a purer and freer atmosphere."

When I reflect on a lifetime, it is easy for me to accept that my beliefs could have been limitations. I seemed to fear being successful and being all I was capable of being. A challenge for me was to create more supportive and less fearful beliefs. John Kehoe in his book, *Mind Power Into the 21st Century: Techniques to Harness the Astounding Powers of Thought*, has this to say:

> What is happening right now in your life is not happening to you as a result of chance. Your past consciousness, your past thoughts, have helped to create it. Your "now" has its causes and roots in your past thinking.

He suggests that the quality of life depends upon the quality of a person's thoughts and ideas. He believes that the unconscious holds an abundant supply of new ideas, answers, and solutions. This is a belief held by many people who practise ways of accessing the unconscious or inner self.

However, Dr. Larry Dossey, a physician from the United States who has published books on soul and meaning and medicine, warns of the potential danger in the belief that we are the creators of our entire reality and responsible for anything that happens. This not only sets up feelings of guilt, shame, and failure when things go wrong, but it discounts the mysteries of the unconscious self and its connection to the world. He says that to honour the mysteries of the unconscious self and its connections to the world requires, one must relinquish conscious control. Those who sit beside the bed of a dying person often hear the words *let go*. It seems that attachment to the conscious world needs to be severed in the "letting go" process of dying. However, I believe it would be foolish to think that there are recipes or prescriptive answers at this time.

It was the first night home after a long hospital stay for one of my patients. I will call her Ruth. She lived with one of her daughters and loved her home and garden. Her husband had died some years before, and she had bravely made a new life. I was in the room with her for the night. It was in the early hours of the morning when Ruth called to me and asked me to put the blind up so that she could see the dawn and the garden. She said that she loved to look out on her garden and she hadn't seen it for the many weeks because of her hospital stay. However, Ruth experienced a powerful moment of insight when she realized that, in order to see the dawn, she had first to extinguish the light that was shining on her bedside table.

I am aware that intuitive knowing has played a large part in the way I have lived my life and cared for my patients. Intuition is difficult to describe, as it is irrational and not derived from observation and experiment or from concepts and reason. Intuition is not a part of conscious mind; rather, it comes from the world of dreams and images and cannot be forced. At the time of my mother's death, I was very much on a spiritual quest and was examining Buddhist text and community. "Pain and suffering come with attachment" is one of the teachings that has stayed with me from that time. The mindfulness teacher, Tara Brach, says, rather simply: "If I am suffering my beliefs are not true." For some time I have felt the need to detach from all things in my conscious world and to prepare to join the collective unconscious, as described by Carl Jung. I have been guided to this place of detachment and am keen to go through transition in a gracious and mentoring way. My legacy is not to fear death. Love and fear are two switches that cannot both be on at the same time!

I would like to feel confident at the time of my transition. As I let go with love into the great formless world, what I take with me is karma.

Jack Kornfield, a contemporary writer on Buddhism, has this to say about karma: "Our unfolding is a reflection of the patterns of our lives, which are sometimes described as 'our fate' or 'our Karma.' No matter the apparent speed, we are simply asked to give ourselves to the process."

"Unfinished business" is a phrase coined by Dr. Elisabeth Kübler-Ross and used in her *Life, Death and Transition* workshops. Jack Kornfield also used this phrase in reflecting on karma:

> Traditionally it is said that if we don't honour our unfinished tasks, our karma will remind us, our unresolved conflicts will re-arise; we will be forced to turn toward what we have not faced in ourselves. Put simply, the circumstances of human life will insist on getting our attention. Our falling needs to be honoured along with our rising.

Every action has a reaction. What a person gives out a person receives back. If a watermelon seed is planted, the fruit from the resulting plant will be a watermelon. This is the concept of karma, and for some there is a belief that karmic imprints travel on the soul to the next life. Karma is a unique and personal energy force. It is the collective results of one's actions. The sooner a person recognizes the influence that karma is playing in his or her life, the sooner this energy, if negative, can be healed. It is transformed by spiritual practices such as meditation and resolved through experiences of forgiveness and a loving heart.

In the course of giving supportive care to elderly and dying people, such concepts as purifying karma, life lessons, and unfinished business need to be understood. It is important to honour the mystery of life, and many nurses have been heard to say, "Patients die when they are ready." Certainly experience demonstrates that dying people seem to have some control—conscious or unconscious—as to the time of their death. There are many anecdotes—She waited for my sister to arrive. We had just left her. He waited until after his son's wedding. Mind, spirit, and soul all seem to have an influence on the body. According to medical intuitive Caroline Myss in her book *The Creation of Health: The Emotional, Psychological, and Spiritual Responses that Promote Health and Healing*:

> What the holistic paradigm suggests—and this is the central difference between two views of diseases—is that the "energy" level of the human being, meaning the inner emotional and spiritual world, precedes, and in fact determines, all that is experienced at the physical level of life … Metaphorically speaking, traditional medicine represents the "mind" of healthcare and the holistic approach represents the "heart" of health

Every faith tradition offers prayers and meditations for heart intentions—intention to convey and express feelings. When a person begins to still his or her mind, repressed feelings are permitted to arise. These feelings may be despair, grief, sorrow, anger, fear, restlessness, loneliness, and judgement. A common Christian term for these feelings is "the dark night of the soul." It is a term used to describe a time when a person loses a perceived meaning and purpose in life, and nothing makes sense anymore. It is an experience of losing what was believed to be the spiritual strengths that supported life and propped up inner life. This is a condition which may be referred to as emotional and spiritual pain. There is no easy answer as to how to relieve this suffering. Consider a spiritual practice of choice, yoga, meditation, and a belief in an afterlife in which the process of spiritual growth continues as well as simply receiving unconditional love.

Medications given to manage pain and anxiety may also produce a meditation-like and euphoric state. By freeing repressed feelings through meditation, people can achieve insight, forgiveness, and peace. One patient who was dying said, "Joy, it is all a myth." I have long pondered on what was the myth she was referring to. In the allegory of the cave in Plato's *Republic*, people have lived their whole lives chained in a cave, facing the back wall of the cave. In the cave, they see only flickering shadows that they mistake for reality. In the allegory, the reader is asked to imagine that, if one of the chained men were to be dragged by force up the rough ascent and into the light of the sun, the man would be angry and in pain. This condition would only worsen when the radiant light of the sun temporarily blinded him. In this allegory, the sunlight represents a new reality that the freed person is experiencing. First of all, he can see only shadows. Gradually, as his eyes become more accustomed to the light, he can see the reflections of people and things in water, and then later he can see the people and things themselves. Eventually he is able to look at the stars and moon, and his perception of the world is forever changed. The freed man would bless himself for this new perspective on the world and pity the other prisoners who have not seen what he is excited to have seen. There would be a desire to bring his fellow cave dwellers out of the cave so that they too could see what he is seeing. If he returned now that his eyes were accustomed to the light, he would be blind when he re-entered the cave—just as he was when first exposed to the light. The prisoners could infer from the returning man's blindness that the journey had harmed him and that they should not undertake a similar journey. They would resist and fight (or kill) anyone who attempted to drag them out of the security and known environment of the cave. People who are dying also face an unknown and may also resist stepping into an unknown. It is my experience that end of life is made easier by having faith in the light that is being described.

This story has many layers of meaning beyond the literal—as do all myths, metaphors, and allegories. Carl Jung spoke of archetypes as images, patterns, and symbols that rise out of the collective unconscious. They appear in dreams, mythology, and fairy tales and describe the patterns of energy which take on form. The archetype of the healer is seen when a person becomes a channel for the ultimate creative force which many of us call God. A frequent mantra I say is "Thy will, not my will." Upon rising, I ask, "What do I need to do today?" I first heard of Plato's cave on an "Epic Tour" of Greece led by Jean Houston in 2014. In telling us this story, she suggested that the light in this allegory is the larger universe which meditators and mystics discover, and the way to turn around a belief is through education and becoming more conscious. She suggested that, at first, it may be difficult to see the larger reality, but with understanding and learning, a person is able to live in the light of this larger reality. In my personal experience of the dream world, I have been given a glimpse of what Plato and Jung are attempting to describe. I have had very colourful visions of landscapes and a sense of travelling vast distances in dreams.

Florence Nightingale, who translated the metaphysical work of Plato as a young woman, wrote, "This world is just a reflection of a greater reality." I can understand that the forms of this world are compressed energy and agree with Florence Nightingale that the purpose of life is to come from imperfection to perfection by becoming more conscious.

From the Indian sage, Ramana Maharshi:

> Meditation is your true nature. You call it meditation now, because there are other thoughts distracting you. When these thoughts are dispelled, you remain alone— that is, in a state of meditation, free from thoughts; and that is your real nature, which you are now trying to gain by keeping away other thoughts.

Common meditation practices focus on breathing. They may be combined with a visualization or with a slow mindful walking technique. I have been asked to make a recording that will assist in a person's transition from this world to the next. This is difficult to do because each person will respond to different visual images, different sounds, and different voices in a way that taps into his or her personal unconscious. I suggest it is more important to be that non-judgemental person at the bedside who follows his or her intuition as to the most helpful support to give the person who is dying. For some, the comfort will come from loving touch like the heart and hand connection taught in therapeutic touch. In this method, the person at the bedside holds the dying person's hand with one hand and places the other hand lightly over the heart and connects with the breath. Others may be comforted with the music from Taize, and some others want to hear "My Way," the song popularized by Frank Sinatra in 1969.

My Way

And now, the end is near
And so I face the final curtain.
My friend, I'll say it clear
I'll state my case, of which I'm certain.
I've lived a life that's full
I've travelled each and every highway.
But more, much more than this
I did it my way ...

Personally, I would like to hear Elton John singing "Candle in the Wind" as well as meditating to Taizé chants and imagining being a particle in the creative void of eternal spaciousness or a cell in the one consciousness.

Beliefs around the meaning of life and death vary among religions and their various interpretations. For Buddhists, there is a belief in rebirth or reincarnation. For many people of Eastern and Western faiths, there is a belief that having a clear mind at the time of death is important. A person with faith in Islam, Christianity, or Judaism, takes comfort in the prayer, "From God we are, to him we return." Others believe that heaven and hell are projections of a person's beliefs, imagination, and own experience. Dr. Elisabeth Kübler Ross described death as a transition when a soul receives "all knowledge" in the process of a life review. The idea of survival of the soul after death appears in many cultures in folklore, mythology, and spiritual writings.

The spiritual dimension of a person is, for some health professionals, the most difficult to define. More and more they are expected by those in their care to have skills in this area. The role of clergy at the bedside is diminishing. Dr. Richard Lamerton, who is a palliative care doctor in the UK, had this to say:

There is That of God in every man.

To That we respond with the desire to serve the weakest and most helpless of our fellows—those who are dying.

Because of That, we should accord freedom and profound dignity …

Good care of a dying person makes his body a comfortable enough place to live in so that he is free, if he wishes, to prepare for death, mentally and spiritually.

Thomas Merton, an American Trappist monk, writer, mystic, poet, social activist, and student of comparative religion, in his writings, conveys the thought that the self that begins is not the self that arrives. The self that begins changes and dies along the way until in the end "no one" is left. This "no one" is our true self or soul, which in esoteric and Eastern philosophy travels from lifetime to lifetime learning lessons and being purified.

What leaves the body at the time of death is energy. Energy can never be destroyed and is seen by some traditions to carry the soul particles from the seen world to the unseen world.

You Cannot Die is the title of a book written by Ian Currie, and the following quote is found in *The Meaning of Death* by John Bowker:

Few people are aware that death, man's most ancient, mysterious and relentless adversary, has been studied systematically over the past century by research scientists working in a variety of fields. Even fewer are aware that the harvest of this effort has been a host of fascinating discoveries which lead to four inescapable conclusions: Human beings do survive physical death; they continue to exist after death at varying levels of awareness and creativity, in a realm that normal human beings cannot normally perceive; this realm is periodically left when the individual takes on a new body, at which time all memory of it, and of former lives is erased; successive re-embodiments do not occur at random, but appear to be linked by a mysterious and fascinating law of causation. These conclusions are stupendous. Their implications are awesome. And they are solidly based on scientific research.

Australian born Dr. Ruth Cilento practised as a holistic physician and is the author of *Heal Cancer—Choose your own survival path*. She writes this about energy:

> The Life Force (Chi, Ka, Prahna) is recognised and heeded in most enlightened cultures of the world. It is not just energy; it is the part of us that enjoys. It is the love, the affection, the perseverance, the hope and the kindness which is inherent in us all. To lose it is to lose the will to live. It is not only a measure of success for a person to survive physically, it is also a matter of growing in spirit, love and understanding, becoming close to God, the Source, or whatever you call that universal energy which is part of each one of us and of which we are all a part.

CHAPTER SEVEN

Caring for Self and Others

This was a most important aspect of my practice, and like many people, I learned from experience and many failures. During a course on neuro-linguistic programming (NLP), I learned to interpret the word *criticism* as merely *feedback*. I would also tell myself that one cannot please all the people all of the time—if we please half of the people half of the time we are doing well. In a palliative care practice, there are many emotions and feelings to consider. I would remind my carers that emotions are felt in the body and feelings are understood in the mind. One of my early lessons was to appreciate that the mind and body are connected. I could appreciate that my sweaty palms before a game of golf were the result of anxiety. The more my mind churned, the sweatier I felt. To heal is to learn and to understand.

I have learnt that I need to have more balance in my life, and I need to look after my energy, which involves all aspects of life. I liked to reflect on what one author, whose name I have forgotten, described as the positive emotions that make a person feel good. They are:

Amusement—We need to laugh in order to release endorphins which, like tears, are nature's "morphine." Laughter, fun, and games are an important part of the emotional diet.

Acceptance—We need to "belong," to associate ourselves with others whose aims and values are similar to our own. We all need to feel that we are accepted as an equal in a group.

Appreciation—This includes appreciation of all our differences. We also need to feel needed and that we have a particular contribution to make. We are like pieces of a jigsaw puzzle which are all different shapes and sizes, and colours, but without everyone, the picture would be incomplete. If we were all just alike, it would be a very dull and uninteresting world.

Affection—This is the recognition that the happiness of other people is important to us. Genuine concern for others is part of the caring profession.

Achievement—This is the realization that we have succeeded in doing something we started out to do. We need to feel that we have accomplished something by our effort and that our lives have had purpose and meaning. I often asked a person at the end of his or her life "How do you want to be remembered?"

I know that I and, possibly, the carers I worked with were often reluctant to admit that we ourselves had needs. We were often encouraged to empower others but not each other. Self-care requires discipline and self-regulation and accepting self-responsibility. When asked about how I cared for myself, I would often reply that, if I could not care for myself—I could not care for others. Yes, there were times when professional and personal boundaries were blurred in the therapeutic partnership with the family in my care. Little acts of kindness such as sending Christmas cards to each other continued for many years. I have always been aware of my diet and have probably spent a small fortune on supplements over the years. It was important for me to realize that

I did not have all the answers. I have always appreciated massage and have had many in the countries I have visited. I particularly remember one given to me by a blind Taiwanese man in a garden setting on the South China Sea on one of my visits to East Malaysia. After the massage, I felt so light. Today I value solitude and meditating and enjoy playing the card game of bridge with old friends from before my leap into being a private palliative care nurse. Books, films, and theatre have been treasured experiences.

There were many difficult times when I had to cease employing a person whether it be an office worker or a person in the role of a palliative care assistant. I am sorry for the times when this could have been accomplished more skilfully. The Enneagram animal I associate with is the tiger, and I have needed to be reminded that the tiger has big paws, so I must tread carefully. On reflection, I have "walked on" people but know that I have also got the job done. It is said that practice makes perfect. Whatever other strategies I have used to avoid stress, the most important has been to have a faith in a higher power and a prayer life. I stopped attending church many years ago, but as my walks took me past a cathedral, I would go in a light a candle and say a private prayer for my family and special friends. To this day I take comfort in lighting candles with the intention of bringing light to what is troubling my mind. Today, as I can see the "big eighty" looming, I take comfort in the fact that my doctor tells me that I am healthier at this time in my life than I was when I first visited him some twenty years ago.

Thomas Huble, in his webinars, talks about two kinds of stress. There is stress which has its source in the unconscious, and there is stress which comes when the future beckons. From a spiritual perspective, the later stress benefits from a response that says "I'm here and I'm available." In my own life, I can reflect on the traumas I buried in the unconscious as a child and appreciate how similar situations experienced today can still cause stress. I feel stress while watching the experiences of war, especially as they are inflicted on children. I also experience stress when I consider what I might be asked to contribute with regard to the greater good in the future. I want to be able to say "I'm here and

I'm available." I certainly responded in that way when asked to go to Malaysia.

In my practice, each situation or case was different with regard to the patient, family members, and friends as well as members of the caring team. There were times when a debriefing session was invaluable. An incident report might need an immediate response. If a problem or an issue was not acknowledged, resolved or aired, rumour and distortions could make a mountain out of a molehill, with unfortunate consequences. This is what happened towards the end of my role as case coordinator. I was away when one of my long-time patients, who was in her late eighties and blind, had a serious fall and broke her pelvis. The carer who was in charge at the time reported information about her condition and the medications that were ordered by a palliative care doctor to distant family members with unfortunate consequences and misunderstandings. It was the policy for members of the caring team to report only to the case coordinator. Ventilation of feelings and questions were encouraged. These included:

- Why am I upset?
- Why am I angry?
- Why am I scared and anxious?
- Why am I sad?
- Why do I feel guilty?
- Why do I feel hurt?
- Why do I feel threatened?
- Why do I feel unrewarded?
- Why don't I feel included?
- What lessons were learnt?
- Is there someone to thank or forgive?
- Is there someone to praise?
- What is true for all persons involved?

When providing care for self and others, I found it invaluable to have an understanding of the Myers Briggs Typology Indicator. My type is the idealist, and I have a temperament that combines intuition and feeling I am interested in personal growth and improving the world. I am also interested in becoming self-actualized and reaching my potential with a "thy will" attitude. In a debriefing session, I would be interested to know the impact a critical incident would have on my practice. I valued autonomy, cooperation, harmony, and self-determination. As an extrovert, I wanted to talk to think and respond to the external energy in the debriefing session. As a feeling person, I would tend to decide with my heart and be inclined to take a personal view. I was learning to develop my thinking as a processing tool and to take a longer, more rational view of situations.

This body of work built on the pioneering work of Jung, and made it more understandable and practical in people's lives. Jung believed that each human being has a specific nature and calling which is uniquely his or her own. In brief, Jung distinguished two general attitudes—introversion and extraversion—and four functions—thinking, feeling, sensing, and intuiting. For example:

- The extrovert has an attitude that is outer directed with a need to be sociable. He or she chooses activities outside the self as a source of energy. The extrovert is often action oriented.
- The introvert has an attitude that is inner directed with a need for privacy and space. The introvert chooses solitude to recover energy and to process ideas.
- The thinking function makes decisions that are logical and evaluates cause and effect. This function may be viewed as cool, distant, direct, and questioning.
- The feeling function is creative and warm. It is people orientated and makes decisions from a heart perspective.
- The sensing function collects information using the five senses. It is good at observing detail and facts in present time.
- The intuitive function sees many possibilities in situations, is influenced by hunches, and is impatient with earthy details. It may be seem to be impractical and to lack grounding. Intuition is an irrational knowing of realities and has its origins in the unconscious.

I learned, from studying the Myers-Briggs Typology, that scheduling visits for my caring team was best left to a sensate person who was good at detail and exploring possibilities. As an extrovert, intuitive, feeling person with a preference to get the work done before play, I have the temperament of an idealist. Myers and Briggs added two more traits to Jung's work on personality types. The two traits were perceiving and judging. A judging trait in the personality profile is good at completing a project and being decisive, while a perceiving trait is good at exploring options and meeting deadlines at the last minute.

While I could attend to computerized accounting and bank reconciliation, these were not my favourite occupations, and I needed to complete them while my mind was fresh. I delegated functions that I found to be stressful to an employee who was skilled and trusted to do that work. My intuitive personality favours cooking with imagination and changing "the recipe" or looking for new ways to achieve a task. People who are sensate follow a "recipe" in detail. To do accounting, my intuitive personality needed to be disciplined and able to adopt a sensate attitude and be in the present moment. The typology developed sixteen personality types, and I found it a valuable guide in the understanding of myself and others.

To achieve what Jung called individuation, or wholeness of the soul, there needs to be a coming together of what is conscious, what is unconscious, and the ability to access the collective unconscious. My spiritual path is to recognize the functions that I avoid and to develop these functions with the intention of becoming more integrated.

Another tool for self-awareness, which I experienced many times, is the Enneagram. The Enneagram is a powerful approach to understanding the psychology, emotions and behaviour of ourselves and others. It has its origins in ancient wisdom traditions and is designed to assist people to pay attention to their primary drives, passions, and compulsions. On a circular diagram, there are nine numbers which are divided into three centres. One group of three numbers represents a heart centre, another group of three numbers represents a head centre, and a third represents the gut centre. This subtle and complex nine-pointed tool gave me the awareness that my "boss" or "challenger" self in the eight-gut centre would benefit from moving to the two in heart centre and working to assist the community at large. This meant that I would be more open and reveal my vulnerability and by so doing would become more concerned for others and more loving. When, as an eight, I move to the positive side of the five-head centre, I see things from a more objective point of view and think more before acting. I have at times moved to the negative side of the five-head centre and felt defeated, thinking that everything I wanted to achieve was too difficult, causing me to become depressed.

I encouraged "I" statements, knowing that when people are encouraged to use "I" statements they begin to take their own needs more seriously. Also "I" messages are a non-aggressive means of expressing one's feelings. Documentation of relevant facts was of paramount importance, and procedures were clearly defined. Advice was sought from outside sources when appropriate. Confidentially was central to my way of care. We honoured patient and staff birthdays in the monthly newsletter. Unwittingly I once included a year of birth, and I received a reminder about confidentiality from a family member. The monthly newsletter, called *The Link*, was also a reminder of anniversaries. The first anniversary of a death was a special time when a card was sent to family members. On occasions, the relationship was particularly close. At these times, family members and caring team members would be invited to share refreshments in the office. Attending funeral services was also an important part of self-care, and we attended in our own time. Bereavement support was informal and initiated on a case-by-case basis by the nurse coordinator.

One grieving relative found comfort following the death of her sister by using the "empty chair" technique. This technique, which had been taught to her by her palliative care nurse, was first popularized by Fritz Perls, one of the founders of Gestalt therapy. In a quiet moment, this young woman would place an empty chair facing her on the other side of a small table where they had shared last days. She would imagine her sister still sitting in the chair she had placed opposite her and would question her regarding the ongoing care of her children or maybe just say to her how much she was missed, or she might reminisce on their childhood. Then she would swap chairs and, in the stillness of her mind, "hear" her sister's replies. Another woman who was missing her husband who had died told me that she slept in his pyjamas when she wanted to be close to him. Others have told me that they still set a place at the table for the one they miss. Those in private care were used to solving their own self-care needs or consulting with people they knew and trusted. They were seldom interested in bereavement support groups.

Self-care required reflective practice and identifying training needs or policy issues that might need to be changed or modified. There were times when a number of close deaths, by necessity, put unresolved grief on hold. A Tibetan monk once said that, to be effective, we need to let our container for emotional involvement become full. However, there is a need to "pull the plug on the well of grief" in order to return to health. The need for self-care was brought home to me in a powerful way. One day I was lying on some large rocks at the beach and looking up at the sky. I saw two sea gulls flying about two metres apart and in parallel flight paths. This continued as far as I could see. When I completed a Reiki II course, my teacher told us to observe the signs in nature for messages. On returning home, I accidently bumped a bedside table, and out flew a small booklet, which landed on the floor. The booklet was on Buddhism, and on the red cover were two parallel white lines. The words between the lines read "You are Responsible." I am responsible— no one else—for my own self-care!

This was a time in my life when I felt very stressed and overwhelmed with the responsibilities of work and young grandchildren and just wanted to stop my work. Then I had an experience that got me back on track. I was living in a two-storey town house, and the floors were connected with a rather steep spiral staircase. It was early morning, and I was wearing slippers and carrying the glass that held my overnight drink of water. As I reached where the steps narrowed to form the spiral, I slipped and crashed to the bottom of the stairs. The glass went flying but did not break. In a state of shock, I picked myself up. There were no broken bones, and what I took to be a paranormal sign was the fact that I had not even bruised. Normally I bruise with the slightest bump. The message I received was that I was turning a corner and out of control, but I (and my work) would be okay.

Guidance from the unseen world came again just recently. I was walking home from a visit to the Botanic Gardens listening to a guided meditation on my iPod, when I suddenly tripped and fell. I struck the pavement, and my iPod and bag went flying. No one else was in sight, and I wondered how I would get up. Just then a young man appeared. He said that his brother, who had been driving their car, saw me fall and told him to go and help me. Imagination or not, but I again felt that this help was not a coincidence. I have lived alone for more than twenty years and consider that I am living by faith rather than fear. I love my freedom and getting to know my shadow parts and doing something that is benevolent and light. I like the following wisdom from a seventy-four-year-old physician and acknowledge that my age has something to do with this state of mind.

> I should like to make a plea that death in the old should be accepted as something always inevitable and sometimes as positively desirable. Once I reach the stage of pre-death, all I ask is that I go on to the end with as much dignity and as little pain as possible—length of further survival becomes immaterial.

However we perceive the journey of life, I strongly believe that we need to walk *with* people on their journey and not take over their journey for them. This is where ethical principles provide guidance. The four main ethical principles are:

Autonomy—respecting individual rights and the right to refuse treatment

Non-maleficence—doing no harm, passively or actively

Beneficence—doing good and being an effective advocate

Justice—being fair to members of the caring team as well as to the unit of care

In addition to the four main ethical principles are four rules to assist in discerning "best action":

Fidelity—keeping promises, being trustworthy

Veracity—telling the truth in a way that is understood

Confidentiality—keeping secrets as well as respecting confidential patient records

Privacy—maintaining dignity and integrity

When considering legal issues in palliative care, which are a most important part of self-care as well as patient care, the principle of double effect is a valuable guide. It hinges on the intention of treatment. Is the intention of the treatment to end life or to relieve pain and distress?

Care is a much better word than *help*. People may say that they do not want anyone to "help" them, but they will usually accept all the care that is available. 'Help suggests that you know more than they do, that you are more together than they are, that you will load them down with all your good advice, and that you will do things differently for them. Remembering little details like making a bed in a particular way or setting a table just so can make or break a caring relationship. I appreciated the fact that, when people look for someone to care for them, they will be looking for someone who will listen to them and will not know what is best for them but will recognize personal preferences and ways of living. It was not appropriate for carers to take up their positions with "maps and guidelines" and all the wonderful things that they had just learned in a course that they had just completed.

When it came to looking after my back, which was damaged from nursing in the era before lifting equipment and slide sheets, I found myself frequently in the kneeling position. Bending over a bed or chair to attend to a nursing task was to be avoided, and rather than recommend a hospital bed which would be more comfortable for me, I respected the fact that most people feel most secure in their own familiar bed. I listened to many married couples who wanted to share their last days and nights in the same bed. I also was aware of others who needed a break from the responsibility of caring and very much needed a good night's sleep. The bereavement period is not easy in itself, and going into this period requires stamina and feelings of "no regrets." There were times when a person who was dying would be near death and then have a good day. I would suggest that the person was having a dress rehearsal. This pattern might occur many times, but a good day often preceded the final breath.

Carers bring themselves to their work. That is why they need to "brush up" their own lives before attempting to "brush up" the lives of another. It is not possible to give away something that a carer does not have himself or herself. For example, those who are reluctant to look at the grief and loss in their own lives will be able to provide little benefit to another. Those who are unable to appreciate their own gifted personalities will have a difficult time appreciating the uniqueness of a bereaved person. The need is to see, in a person's own mind's eye, a person with dignity and worth, even if their "now" living conditions are not the best—to see beyond the chaos and see the real person rather than surroundings. There may be times when the carer just needs to "be" there, not to do anything apart from being calm and peaceful. One member of my team was very good at doing this. However other team members were prone to get upset when things were not done—like leaving unwashed dishes in the sink.

By understanding and being in touch with their own personal experience, people giving support at the end of life will know not to say "I know how you feel" because it is not possible for another human being to know how another person feels. It is appreciated when a person tries to understand how the other person is feeling, or to know how they would feel if they were in their position. Most of all, people want carers who *listen* to them, not with their heads, but with their hearts. Repressed feelings include anger at an event in childhood or during a person's lifetime when he or she felt powerless to defend himself or herself or to change a situation. Repressed feelings include grief that was "put on hold" and not processed and worked through—as I did with my own grief after my father died. When my father died, I had two small children, and we were planning to move from Rochester, New York, to Adelaide, South Australia. My husband had a position with the School of Dentistry at the Adelaide University. This university paid for our airfare to return to Australia. While we lived in Adelaide, I had two more children, and the eldest of my four children was just five years old. I had no family or old friends for support, and I learned to care for myself.

While I survived the early years of bringing up children in a difficult situation, the memories of exhaustion remained buried in my psyche only to surface when I was asked to babysit my young grandchildren. I had my children in the era when a father's role did not include hands-on baby care. In the hospice philosophy, the expression "wounded healer" is used. People are able to connect at a deeper level through the sharing of their wounds. However, it is not appropriate for those in a caring role to seek solace from their patients. I used to say to the caring team that we are in the therapeutic relationship primarily to meet the needs of others. Yes, there can be a blurring of lines, and it is important to have a healthy sense of self. Princess Diana's life is an example of unconscious wounds being made conscious. Hurts from life events left her feeling disillusioned, misunderstood, and powerless from lack of support from people she trusted. People from all walks of life could recognize those feelings—hence the outpouring of shared grief. It is common for those caring, as well as for those who are cared for, to have wishes and prayers that have never been fulfilled.

"Quality of life" is another term frequently used when terminal care issues are being considered. This term is said to reflect the difference—or gap—between the hopes and expectations of a person and his or her present experience. On a different level, I can relate to wisdom from Stephen Levine, the author of *Who Dies?: An Investigation of Conscious Living and conscious Dying*. He writes, with regard to hope, that when a person is living in the "present moment," fears are removed, and there is no need for hope. Mindfulness is more commonly being introduced into general medical practice. This is an example of how those who work in palliative care could benefit from introducing a spiritual approach into their care. Stephen Levine writes that all fear has an element of resistance and a leaning away from the moment, and that its dynamic is not unlike that of strong desire, except that fear leans backward into the last safe moment while desire leans forward toward the next possibility of satisfaction. Each lacks the peace to be found in.

> Reason says, "I will beguile him with the tongue;"
> Love says, "Be silent. I will beguile him with the soul."

> — Rumi

Listening to and being with a person in a calm state is the basis for all care. It is an art and an intuitive process to listen to what is not being said. What is considered to be good manners and a stiff upper lip can mask true feelings. Death is a portal into what people who have had a near-death experience call "the light." It is a time when honesty is usually appreciated rather than an affirmative "yes" that is followed by an excuse at a later date. It is also important for the person being cared for to be able to say no without the fear of being deserted and without offence being taken. I have encountered many patients who dutifully take medications to please their doctor or family members and maybe fear that a refusal of treatment will be followed with a lack of interest. There is a real poverty in any relationship if either person is not comfortable in saying no.

When asked during an interview, "How do you prepare someone to die?" Dr. Viktor Frankl, the noted Viennese psychiatrist, replied, "I wouldn't venture to prepare anyone else to die, unless I had first prepared myself. My patients know exactly when what I say is authentic and when it is not."

The health team is there, primarily, to meet other people's needs. We all need to be needed. It is part of our very existence, but we need to understand how to meet our own needs and not to expect others to meet them for us. This is where we can get into trouble and feel hurt, rejected, and unloved. Those who give to themselves first have so much more to give to others. The example of the oxygen mask dropping down in an aeroplane is often cited as a metaphor for this idea. So the first lesson a carer (we are all carers in some form or other) needs to learn is self-care. When we are replenished, we give more willingly and never reach that burn-out condition. No one can make another person happy, sad, or angry. How we respond or react is a choice.

Mahatma Gandhi summed up his life philosophy when a friend asked him if his aim in settling in the village and serving the villagers as best he could was purely humanitarian. Gandhi replied, "I am here to serve no one else but myself, to find my own self-realization through service to these village folk."

Counsellors, psychiatrists, psychologists, social workers, and ministers of religion are all counted among those whose formal role is to be with people in managing distressing life events.

There are common traps to be avoided:

- Enjoying the control or power and influence over someone
- Being empowered by ego flattery and being emotionally blackmailed
- Becoming stressed—being drained and exhausted to the point of ill health
- Feeling unrewarded and not seeming to make a difference
- Having difficulty in saying no and in setting realistic boundaries
- Falling into psychological traps transference, projection, and co-dependency

There are strategies you can employ:

- Know your own capabilities and when you can make a difference and when you cannot
- Reflect deeply on your soul's purpose and sacred contract
- Give yourself self-care and appreciation
- Become familiar with your temperament and psychological type. This self-knowledge will give you an appreciation of situations that will stress you when you are not using your preferred way

of responding to a situation and also what situations nurture and promote relaxation. As well as considering temperament and psychological type, there is a lifetime of coping skills to consider. Coping skills are related to personal beliefs and values. It may be helpful to reflect on the ways you have lived your life to this time and to determine what has worked for you and what has not worked for you. Do you address problems as they arise or do you have a tendency to avoid responsibility for them? Are you secure within yourself? What patterns of behaviour work for you, and which ones do you need to avoid or change?

There are factors that lead to a lack of self-care and appreciation

- People who work in the caring profession may be reluctant to admit that they themselves have needs.
- They may be unable to balance a multi-faceted life and feel that their work defines them as individual people.
- They may neglect the need for a well-balanced diet, adequate sleep and regular exercise. Self-pampering activities need not carry guilt.
- Carers may experience an unmanageable blurring of personal and professional boundaries.
- They may not be in the habit of practising time management and the skills needed to distinguish a priority.
- They may fear rejection and loss of respect from other team members if they show weakness or need.
- Debriefing can be viewed as threatening or critical of personal performance. If carers have training in self-awareness, they will know that, although they cannot change circumstances, they do have the power to change their attitude to those circumstances. What is perceived as criticism can be viewed as feedback.
- Carers often do not understand that self-care requires discipline, self-regulation, and self-responsibility.
- Events that strengthen team building and celebrating life's milestones may be missing.

My experience was that holistic care was comprehensive care. It required the person providing the care to be mindful, present in the moment, patient, and not in need of answers and quick solutions. It required, the carer must accept the existence of mystery and must realize that the soul has its own life and sends thoughts to the mind for our own welfare. It was important to always have an intention to care in a way that supported the highest good.

As a gift to myself, I spent a weekend retreat with art therapist Greg Furth when he visited Sydney one year. I knew of his connection with Elisabeth Kübler-Ross and was keen to meet him. The workshop title was "My Mother." I thought I had reflected deeply on my relationship with my own mother, but found the retreat illuminating. We were asked to do two drawings of our mother—one as we remembered her and another one of our "wished-for" mother. In the first drawing, I drew my mother sitting at her organ playing. There was a vase of flowers on top of the organ. She loved flowers. The setting was homely. In the second drawing, I depicted, not an organ, but a piano, and the furniture was antique and elegant. A woven carpet graced the floor. As a child, I related the organ to church and, even at a young age, I must have been rebellious about an association with organized religion. Another exercise we did was to place our mothers in our mind's eye and, with our non-dominant hand, write a message from her. My scrawling handwriting produced words of suffering and sorrow, and I felt connected in a way I had not before experienced in real life.

Caring for self is not easy; it encompasses many levels of understanding.

CHAPTER EIGHT

Wisdom from the Hospice Philosophy

The World Health Organization Definition of Palliative Care 2011 states:

> Palliative care is an approach that improves the quality of life of patients and their families facing the problem associated with life-threatening illness, through the prevention and relief of suffering by means of early identification and impeccable assessment and treatment of pain and other problems, physical, psychosocial and spiritual. Palliative care:

- provides relief from pain and other distressing symptoms;
- affirms life and regards dying as a normal process;
- intends neither to hasten nor to postpone death;
- integrates the psychological and spiritual aspects of patient care;
- offers a support system to help patients live as actively as possible until death;
- offers a support system to help the family cope during the patient's illness and in their own bereavement;
- uses a team approach to address the needs of patients and their families, including bereavement counselling, if indicated;

- will enhance quality of life, and may also positively influence the course of illness;
- is applicable early in the course of illness, in conjunction with other therapies that are intended to prolong life, such as chemotherapy or radiation therapy, and includes those investigations needed to better understand and manage distressing clinical complications.

In my nurse practice, I appreciated guidance from this definition and endeavoured to find a balance between Eastern and Western traditions and values. Western traditions tend to have excellence in science and technology. By combining this knowledge with the sensitivity of energy work and honouring the need for balance in all things, we brought the benefits from both traditions together to enhance the healthcare and well-being of the elderly and dying. It was my intention to integrate the practice of palliative care with gerontology (healthy ageing) and to give consideration and respect to people from different backgrounds, cultures, and different world views. It is recognized that traditions about "breaking bad news" and about family interactions may differ in Western and Eastern environments and in indigenous cultures. For example, in some Eastern cultures, it is considered to be a kindness to protect people who are facing a life-threatening illness from bad news. In such cases, families and health professionals express their care and concern in other loving and intuitive ways that seek to protect rather than inform. This may be seen as paternalism in a Western culture where there are legal requirements of disclosure and informed consent. In an Eastern setting, it may be seen as a burden to inform patients that they have life-threatening illnesses. There is a need for ethical considerations as well as legal requirements, and a generalization cannot be made based on religion, cultural norms, and education. With modern global interactions, those influences cross traditional boundaries.

In spite of the multiple losses and hardships suffered by the Australian Aborigines, there is a growing respect by non-indigenous Australia for Aboriginal culture and ceremonies. Ceremonies around death may include transporting a dying person home to the place of birth. It may be important for the place of death to be smoked to purify it of bad spirits. Sensitivity to cultural considerations is of paramount importance in healthcare generally, and in palliative care particularly.

> It may be considered impolite or offensive to look directly at an Indigenous person. It will be difficult for an Indigenous person to question a doctor's management, even if it is clearly impractical. Health decisions tend to be a family or community affair. Family structure is complex and governed by recognised obligations and cultural rules.
>
> —Emeritus Professor Ian Maddocks, AM

Values common to all include integrity, honesty, respect, trust, responsibility, humility, service to another, compassion, and love. Decisions are best be made using empathy. Empathy involves trying to understand how a person experiences a situation and communicating this understanding clearly to another person. It means trying to sense exactly what another person is feeling. We attempt to walk in the other person's shoes and to feel *with* the person rather than *for* him or her, which is sympathy.

I have had an interest in Native American indigenous cultures as well as Australian indigenous culture. The following has been written especially for me by Helen Parer, who is a Roman Catholic nun. Helen's involvement in palliative care goes back to the early influence of her mother, who was matron of a hospital, and her three uncles, who were doctors. Helen taught and worked with me during the formative years of my nurse practice. Her interests and studies have been in the areas of education, English as a second language, psychology, and pastoral care. She studied pastoral studies and Jungian psychology in Australia and Chicago in the United States. This is what she has to say about the Indigenous people of Australia:

The indigenous people of Australia are the custodians of a very old culture which embraces such things as knowledge, belief, morals, and customs. It is our cultural beliefs that give meaning and purpose to our lives—our culture is the very air that we breathe. With a few exceptions the indigenous people of Central Australia, Northern Australia and Western Australia are still strongly influenced by, and aware of their systems of social, economic, mythological and ritual values despite the different languages, customs and practices. The Centralia Australian People, the Tiwi People, The Cape York People and the Torres Strait Island people each have a separate belief yet share much in common. To speak of all Indigenous people as "one" is impossible.

Because of the way Australia was invaded, the indigenous people generally, have not trusted newcomers sufficiently to share their beliefs and traditions with them so that we need to be particularly sensitive and attentive to the family members and give them permission to do the things they need to do. Death is a social event; the removal of a member of society from their accustomed place. Like all people the family members want to know what the medical staff think is happening. When a person is dying people watch nearby or at a distance, according to the relationship rules of the group and depending on the non-indigenous influences over the years. It is taboo in Aboriginal culture to ask questions, you learn by observation and listening. The family may feel powerless in the presence of modern medicine or they may feel very powerful and feel they can help the person better than modern medicine and this could be true as they have a deep spirituality and an extensive knowledge of bush medicine and treatment. We need to believe in them and support them.

It is alien for a traditional person to die in hospital—
the preferable place is on their land. If a person dies
in hospital, the place where the person died will hold
a special significance. All the places where the person
has been are smoked (cleansed) in the presence of the
family members. Give the people permission to smoke
the area if they want to. The clothes the person was
wearing before they died may need to be given to the
family who in turn will give them to the elders who have
the responsibility to try and resolve what or who caused
the person to die. Visions and dreams play a big part
in their spiritual experiences. The dead person's name
is not mentioned and people with the same name are
addressed by another name.

People's attitudes to death are shaped by many factors including
their experiences, beliefs, and world views. For some, the purpose of
life are well defined and explained in the teachings of their religion; for
others, life and death are mysteries. Historical perspectives all shape
attitudes; these include society's acceptance of death as part of life, a
personal experience, the result of a major disease outbreak, war, and
natural disasters. Fear of death may include fear of dependency, the pain
of the dying process, the indignity, isolation, separation and rejection,
leaving loved ones, after-life concerns, the finality of death, the fate
of the body, being powerless, and feeling overwhelmed. Throughout
a lifetime it is common to dissociate from painful and fearful events
and to have a diminished awareness of them. Dissociation is a mental
process of disconnecting from one's thoughts, feelings, and memories.
Thomas Huble, the mystical teacher, observed that much of the fear
associated with death anxiety may be more correctly related to other
fears that have not been faced.

Whether those facing a life-threatening illness receive supportive
care in a separate purpose-built unit—a separate ward or room in a
hospital, a nursing home—or at home itself, the hospice philosophy of
care may be applied. The philosophy reflects an attitude to care. The

teaching of palliative care principles is now included in many university curricula and in many diverse disciplines within the health professions. A person's primary health professional may be a doctor, nurse, or some other allied health professional. There needs to be respect for, and interaction with, all health team members—from both traditional allopathic and complementary health professionals.

In the age of specialization, it is interesting to remember the roots of the hospice philosophy. The mediaeval hospice was a place of refreshment, rest, and shelter for pilgrims and travellers. All those who reached its doors were cared for until they were ready to continue their journey. This included care of the sick and wounded. When the Irish Sisters of Charity opened Our Lady's Hospice in Dublin in 1846 and St. Joseph's Hospice in London in 1905, they included many long-stay patients but made the dying—those patients on their final journey— their special concern. In my practice, I combined care of the elderly and care of the dying and believe that this approach could assist many nursing home patients approach death more positively.

St. Christopher's, the first purpose-built research and teaching hospice, was opened in London in 1967 by Dame Cicely Saunders who is recognized as the founder of the modern hospice movement. Dame Cicely trained as a nurse, social worker, and doctor to fulfil her calling to care for dying cancer patients. She pioneered the use of morphine in managing cancer pain. These are her words:

> The focus of the modern hospice began with the attention to the nature of terminal pain, to its better understanding and therefore more effective treatment. Alongside this came a revival of the old concept of a 'good death' and attention to the achievement that a patient could still make in the face of physical deterioration.

Each person is unique, and there is no magic formula for dealing with everyone. However, there may be some insights to be gained when the "right" questions are asked. Knowing what to ask is often an intuitive process and demonstrates whether health professionals and carers are secure in themselves—about who they are and what is important to them. Self-awareness and self-knowledge can prevent carers from projecting personal issues and prejudices onto the person receiving care and onto all those involved in the case.

Dr. Balfour Mount, a Canadian surgeon, coined the term *palliative care* in 1975 and established a palliative care service at the Royal Victoria Hospital in Montreal to further define the needs of the terminally ill patients, and to initiate ways of meeting those needs more appropriately within a general hospital setting. The word *palliative*, which means to "cloak" or "hide" comes from the Latin word *pallium*. Dr. Mount said: "It has been a rare privilege to take part in the first tottering steps of an infant discipline." I have been privileged to attend two international conferences on palliative care and one on AIDS in Montreal, Canada.

The conference on AIDS was held in 1989. A message for the conference from Elisabeth Kübler-Ross was that, because of AIDS, the world would become kinder. It is obvious that this is true when it comes to equal rights for same-sex relationships, and in general, there is more understanding and compassion for different sexual orientations. One of the keynote speakers, whose name I have forgotten, mentioned that he was to visit my homeland Australia. There were thousands of participants at the conference, and yet this speaker and I came face to face on a staircase, and I was able to invite him to present for NurseLink in Adelaide. He was a passionate speaker and highlighted the importance of loving relationships for the nurturing of children regardless of gender. Many of the people who were dying from AIDS wanted to have a say in how they died. One young man made a video that documented his last weeks. In the video, he shared his thoughts and fears as well as his insights into his suffering. This was a difficult time to be a parent of a child suffering from AIDS-related illnesses, and the diagnosis was often hidden because of the stigma the disease carried. Then there were questions of an ethical nature to be explored. One of these was the question of confidentiality, and whether the spouse or partner of the person with AIDS had a right to be told of a positive test result. I believe the words of Elisabeth Kübler-Ross at that time have become true, and the world has become kinder with the light of understanding.

In my practice and in the education programs I organized, I was very privileged to have Emeritus Professor Ian Maddocks, AM, support my work. He said that he was happy to work alongside me but not for me—most probably recognizing my "boss" energy and knowing his own calling. The following is an excerpt from a Chapter in *A Passion for Caring—Book 2*. The excerpt was written by Emeritus Professor Maddocks AM:

> The approach, knowledge and skills developed in palliative care for cancer patients are also relevant to the care of many whose advanced and terminal disease is not cancer, but involves organ failure, degenerative disease and dementia, conditions which commonly afflict the elderly and very elderly. The services and institutions that are designed to care for the elderly have not often had the benefit of the resources, the knowledge or the expertise developed in palliative care, but increasingly it is being recognised that these deserve greater expression in aged care.
>
> Palliative care services and aged care must develop appropriately to the needs of each country, and will therefore differ in many respects from place to place. But ageing of communities is a world-wide phenomenon, and whereas in former times a high proportion of deaths occurred in small children, now this is only so in the most deprived and desperate places. Increasingly, death is something seen mainly in old age, and we need to examine whether we are bringing to those senior members of our societies the respect and the care which they deserve in their final illnesses. The comfort of persons with serious and incurable illness is important in every culture.

Powerful examples of the hospice philosophy are to be found worldwide. This example was provided at a nurse healers' conference in New York that I attended in 1991. The presenter was Dorothy Larkin, a US nurse in private practice who was a member of the New York Milton H. Erickson Society for Psychotherapy and Hypnosis. She told the audience, which consisted mainly of nurses, that when Milton Erickson, psychologist and father of modern hypnosis, was a young man, he found that a lost horse had come to his farm. When he returned it to its rightful owner, the owner asked, "How did you know to bring the horse to me?" Erickson replied, "I didn't know—I only had to keep the horse on the road. He knew his own way home."

So it is with the people in our care. In the process of preparing for death, or of healing the psyche, the patient may seek to have curative treatment extended if only for the psychological support of "buying time" or "keeping the horse on the road."

Erik Erikson, the American developmental psychologist and psychoanalyst known for his theory on psychosocial development of the human, stressed that conflicts that occur in early life and are unresolved can be resolved successfully later in life. His wisdom indicated that a benefit of old age is that it gives us a second chance to tackle these issues. He also believed that resolved conflicts may recur and need to be resolved again. "Unfinished business" in those we care for needs to be understood and accepted as part of the process of ageing and dying. An important part of making preparations for end of life is to consider such unfinished business. A trusted listener can be a catalyst in reframing and understanding life events and life experiences. There is power in genuine praise when it is given with a genuine intention. Naomi Feil, the validation therapist, writes that it is normal for very old people to finish life by completing their unfinished past: they struggle to make up, to mend their fences, to express repressed emotions, to make peace. Not all elderly and dying people have access to trained psychologists, and that is why I believe nurses benefit from a basic understanding of these theories. It is the day-to-day interactions that are enriched with an appreciation of basic psychology. We need to have many tools in our toolkit if we are to walk beside a person in the period leading to end of life.

There is a growing interest in validation therapy, which was founded by Naomi Feil. She believes that, unless each of Erikson's life stages are dealt with satisfactorily, the stages can hold a person in a repetitive pattern of behaviour. People with unresolved life tasks sometimes carry these tasks with them into very old age and often use people and symbols in present time to substitute for people in the past in order to unload painful emotions. A woman who was telling me about her family kept repeating the circumstances of the road accident that had killed her son. It was obvious that she had forgotten that she had previously told the story, and by repeating it she was still trying to make sense of the accident in a personally meaningful way. The story was unfinished.

Here are Erikson's stages of development:

1. **Infancy**— The baby learns to get and to give in return. This period is hopefully one of security and trusting in the world. A baby learns to smile and to cry in order to get needs met. The opposite is mistrust, uncertainty, fear and a feeling that life is risky.
2. **Early childhood**—The toddler learns to hold on and to let go. This period is the beginning of independence and being resourceful. It is when the toddler learns to control bowels and bladder. The opposite is being ashamed, exposed, inadequate, and powerless.
3. **Active play age**—The child learns to go after others and to play like others. This stage is lively and expansive. The child is able to question the rules and challenge authority. The opposite is feeling guilty, hostile, hurt, and getting carried away.
4. **School age**—A child learns to complete things and to make things together. He or she is becoming competent, productive, and able to take things in stride. He or she is eager to encounter new situations and new people.

5. **Adolescence**—The young adult learns to be himself or herself and to share being that individual. The young adult becomes comfortable with sex roles and career plans, and also becomes inner-directed and independent.

6. **Young adult**—The young adult is able to lose himself or herself and to find himself or herself in another. The young adult is able to be close, accountable, and accepting of diversity in others, and is willing to abandon self to another and willing to make reasonable demands.

7. **Adulthood**—The adult experience is to be and to take care of. The adult is dependable and protective, willing to try new things, and to be able to negotiate, revise, and renew.

8. **Maturity**—The mature individual's purpose is to be through having been and to face not being.

Erikson's final stage is maturity, when hopefully people experience a sense of accomplishment, pride in their efforts, being useful, involved, optimistic, at home with self and the cosmos, and able to go alone. The opposite to these feelings are disgust; despair; hopelessness; having nothing to strive for or enjoy; feeling bitter about losses; feeling pessimistic about most life circumstances; being unwilling to acknowledge and accept reality or limits; sensing meaninglessness and self-rejection. Whether a person is dying from disease or old age, these stages may be expressed in one form or another.

Here is an example of this incomplete stage: A father was telling the story of his life in the army to his nurse. He told of the time when war ended and he had to return to his wife and children. He had enjoyed the discipline he had experienced in the army and the sense of power it gave him. He expected his wife and children to replace his army colleagues and snap to attention when he gave an order. This attitude sent his children away from home as soon as they were able to leave and be independent. Now, forty years later, this man wanted to ask forgiveness from his son and daughter and to be reunited as he faced the end.

In these stages, the first step is to form a therapeutic relationship based on *trust*. Trust must be the underpinning in one's relationship with one's self, one's care team members, and one's "god." People's happiness and ability to be at peace with themselves depends on their attitude to their circumstances. For some people, a seemingly negative situation, when viewed in a new light, can become something positive. For example, often when people are diagnosed with life-threatening illnesses, they realize that this "jolt" is the opportunity they need to put right many relationships. For a short period, I was a member of Zonta International, which is a global organization of women in business and the professions working together to advance the status of women. It was customary for new members to introduce themselves. So many said that their life had begun with a loss such as divorce or the death of a partner. I know that, if I were still the wife of an orthodontist, I could not have had the experiences and lessons I have had in this last period of my life.

In building trust, it is often necessary to find common ground in the energy fields. One way to discover common ground is to consider the function of each energy centre found in our bodies and to "compare notes." There are seven main energy centres or chakras. When connecting at the level of the base chakra, having had an experience of the same religion can be a starting point in the search for common ground. When connecting at the level of the heart chakra, a shared loss of some kind can be bonding. Recently I was playing a game of bridge, and one of the players asked if any of us believed in extrasensory perception (ESP). I nodded enthusiastically, and she told us about a synchronicity her son had just experienced. It was a moment of togetherness. In order to explore chakras, which have their foundation in ancient Hindu wisdom, I have given brief descriptions based on the work of Caroline Myss, which is available without cost on her website: www.myss.com

> The **base chakra** is connected to family, religion, or "tribe" and is concerned with safety and security and the ability to provide for life's necessities. It is concerned with law and order, bonds and support, and who has authority over a person. It reminds us of the need to consider possible wounds arising from family or representatives of family.

The **sacral chakra** is about creativity, sexuality, and finances. It concerns physical survival, creativity, relationships, and issues of control. It asks: "Can I depend on you?" and "Are you comfortable with my sexuality?"

The **self-esteem chakra** is about accepting the process of becoming and taking self-responsibility. It is about having strong boundaries and being comfortable with one's self and recognizing one's strengths and weaknesses.

The **heart chakra** mediates between the body and soul and determines health, strength, and balance. Love is central to this chakra and motivates body, mind, and spirit. It is concerned with love, hatred, bitterness, grief, anger, jealousy, and healing invisible wounds. It is concerned with forgiveness of self and others.

The **throat chakra** is the centre for communication and involves informed consent, will, choice, and living with consequences. Choice includes living by faith or living by fear. Is there regret for not following a dream and not taking control? Is the person able to say "Thy will, not my will"?

The **brow chakra** is often referred to as the third eye. It is the energy centre of intuition, intellect, and reasoning. It discerns what truth is and what is illusion.

The **crown chakra** connects the energy centres to our spiritual nature and living in the present moment of spacious awareness. It is our personal relationship with the divine.

In the period of separation pending legal divorce, I had an experience of major significance. I had been experiencing severe pain in my left arm from a pinched nerve in my neck. On my way to attend a nurse healers' conference in Sacramento, I took a bus tour through the beautiful valley of Yosemite. In a log cabin surrounded by pine trees, I had a dream in which I could see green forceps trying to mend the outside membrane of a broken butterfly's wing. In the dream, the first forceps were put aside and another pair were brought in to complete the task. On my return to Australia, I went through a series of tests and x-rays looking for a way to relieve this pain. A neurosurgeon offered a procedure that involved a discectomy and bone graft to fuse my C6 and C7 vertebrae. It was just prior to Christmas, and my first Christmas without the presence of family. I was on my own. The first attempt of surgery failed to relieve the pain, as a bony spur was still pinching the nerve. Bravely I agreed to more surgery.

My father had died a quadriplegic, and here I was facing delicate surgery on my spine—not once but twice! Like Elisabeth Kübler-Ross, I found it was the woman who cleaned the room who showed the most empathy and gave the most comfort. A kindly nun came to see me and offered to place the surgeon's name and my name on their altar. I remember placing a torn-out page from a little book on hugs under my ID band before going to the theatre. In reality what was happening, from an energy perspective, was that the area of my throat chakra was being strengthened and supported for the work ahead of me. That was more than twenty years ago, and there have been many lessons to learn since that difficult time in my life.

It was the view of Elisabeth Kübler-Ross that death is an integral part of our lives and gives meaning to it. We should see death, she says, as an invisible, friendly companion to life's journey, reminding us not to put off till tomorrow what should be done today, but to live life fully. Whether we live to eight, eighteen, or eighty, it is the quality of our living that is important. Towards the end of life, the physical body will fail; however, the spirit of the person can be strong, and life can still be lived authentically without pretence.

A good friend, Rita Ward, has received several national awards for her contribution to education on grief and loss. For a time, she coordinated the office and practice in Brisbane while I split my time between Adelaide and Brisbane. We conducted many education sessions together. She was the first Australian counsellor to study with Elisabeth Kübler-Ross in the US, and she shared this quote with me from Elisabeth Kübler-Ross:

> It is denial of death that is partially responsible for people living empty purposeless lives; for when you live as if you'll live forever it becomes easy to postpone the things you know that you must do. You live your life in preparation for tomorrow or in remembrance of yesterday and meanwhile, each today is lost. In contrast, when you fully understand that each day you awaken could be the last you have, you take time that day to grow, to become more of who you really are, to reach out to other human beings.

What choices do people faced with a terminal or life-limiting illness have?

- They can choose to make decisions based on fear or based on knowledge, understanding, and faith in being part of a larger and cosmic world view.
- They can choose to heed the changes in their bodies and listen to their messages or to ignore and deny them.
- They can choose to project or displace their deep fears. Fears about their own death may be expressed in ways that seems to relate to other family members or other people.
- They can choose their attitude and response—find meaning or become despairing, embrace God's will or blame another.
- They can choose attachment or detachment as a way of coping. They may be attached to their ego or sense of who they are in this world and live life viewed through their ego, or they may

detach from ego and live in the present moment of stillness with acceptance.

- They can choose to make decisions based solely on personal beliefs and values, which may be limited, or they can choose to make decisions based on a combination of their personal beliefs and values together with a medical and scientific perspective.
- They can choose acceptance rather than holding onto an energy identity of painful emotions or onto hope that is not based on reality.

Fear acts as a negative magnet. What might people faced with a terminal or life-limiting illness fear?

- The unknown or future
- Being out of control
- Pain and suffering
- Punishment in some form or karmic forces
- Financial burdens of care
- Abandonment by family members, friends, and health professionals
- Not being remembered kindly or for fulfilling their potential
- Loss of their faith

What might people faced with a terminal or life-limiting illness fear have faith in?

- **Signals from the body**: if tired, rest; if hungry, eat a nourishing meal; if stressed, have a relaxing massage; if there is pain or other symptoms, consult the doctor or support therapist. The connectedness of mind, body, and soul facilitates in understanding the messages sourced in the body.
- **Sensing energy levels**. Energy medicine is based on the chakras, which are located along the midline in the body. Chinese medical practitioners call it chi. To Hindu mystics, it is the cosmic energy of Shakti. Subtle shifts in energy affect the

cells of the body. People can visualize and be familiar with their chakras—what parts of the body feel alive and what parts feel dull. Energy medicine's primary function is to remove energy blocks and restore balance.

- **Comfort from a guardian angel, ancestor, or spiritual being**. Inner guidance may draw a person to a workshop or to a particular doctor or healer. Guidance can come in meditation that quietens the mind. There is a need to go to the stillness beyond mind—the mind might be telling us what our feelings and fears should be rather than letting our feelings and fears speak for themselves.

- **Science**. Evidenced-based research assists doctors in eliminating "trial and error." Science and technology go hand in hand to minimize discomforts and promote understanding. Dame Cicely Saunders, the founder of the modern hospice movement, demonstrated that hospice is a combination of heart and science.

- **Dreams**. Dr. Judith Orloff is a practising psychiatrist, intuitive healer and the author of *Dr. Judith Orloff's Guide to Intuitive Healing: 5 Steps to Physical, Emtional, and Sexual Wellness,* and also *Second Sight: An Intuitive Psychiatrist Tells Her Extraordinary Story and Shows You How to Tap Your Own Inner Wisdom.* She says that dreams keep a person well and provide the answers. She says that we are in partnership with our dreams and can dialogue with them. For her, dreaming is a direct line to a place where magic abounds and nothing is without meaning. I believe dreams to be the interface between this world and the next and a way to have a relationship with our inner worlds.

- **Meditation**. There are two types: calm abiding and insight meditation. Calm abiding meditation enables a person to observe thoughts and emotions from afar—like clouds drifting past a clear bright sun in the sky or floating on the breath. An example of insight meditation is stilling the mind by using conscious breathing techniques to gain insight into questions that arise and to offer and receive the eternal power of prayer. Meditation is a doorway into the unconscious.

Here is what *The Tibetan Book of the Dead* has to say about life after death:

> It is not necessary to suppose that all the dead in the Intermediate State experience the same phenomena, any more than all the living do in the human world, or in dreams ... Accordingly, for a Buddhist of some other school, as for a Hindu, or a Moslem, or a Christian, the Bardo experiences would be appropriately different: the Buddhist's or the Hindu's thought-form, as in a dream state, would give rise to corresponding visions of the deities of the Buddhist or Hindu pantheon; a Moslem's, to visions of the Moslem Paradise; a Christian's, to visions of the Christian Heaven, or an American Indian's to visions of the Happy Hunting Ground.

Janet Macrae is a therapeutic touch nurse practitioner and author who practices in the United States. As well as writing her book on therapeutic touch (*Therapeutic Touch: A Practical Guide*) she co-authored a book with Michael D. Calabria entitled *Suggestions for Thought by Florence Nightingale: Selections and Commentaries.* This book contains previously unpublished writings by Florence Nightingale. In the chapter entitled "On Life after Death," Janet Macrae has this to say:

> For Nightingale the question of death was relatively simple: as each individual embodies unique qualities that cannot be duplicated, it would not be consistent with God's benevolent nature to obliterate that being. Because it is God's plan to raise mankind from imperfection to perfection, death must initiate a different mode of existence, one that allows for continued development.

The following case history is full of ritual and symbols that go beyond words. A man, successful in a worldly sense, was dying from cancer when the NurseLink nurse met him. He was tucked up snugly in his own bed, and his every comfort was being attended to by a very beautiful, sensitive, and intelligent second wife. He loved to hear their two children practising their music and making the sounds of their daily activities.

The specialist palliative care doctor came and offered a hospital admission while keeping hope realistic and honest. The patient looked so comfortable in his bed and in atmosphere that would be difficult for any hospital to duplicate. The patient stayed put and settled down to write letters to his friends and four children. The letters to the children (they were in their thirties and pre-teens) were moving and inspiring.

This was followed by a healing visit from his first wife and mother of the two eldest children. This visit, and indeed friendship, was welcomed by the current wife who said, "After all, she has been such an important part of his life." During that night, his life force and cancer drained away (his wife's insight). He died early the next day. During the night, he had been cared for by his eldest son and wife. They had lovingly and constantly cleaned and comforted him.

His eldest daughter, when she arrived in her last hours, matched his breathing with her breath, and that was how he took his final breath. Cleansed and loved! No medical intervention, no drugs—just love! His eldest son and a male extended family member washed, shaved, and dressed his body. His wife shampooed his hair. He lay for most of the day, still and noble, in his bed. Close family members kept vigil and shed tears in remembrance. He left the house via the front door and front gate with an honour guard of family and extended family members. It was wonderful to see and experience. His funeral was personalized and truly a celebration of his life. It included the reading of the letter to friends.

I feel that we, as a society, and especially as those who walk the journey with dying people, still have much to learn. Death is a great teacher for the art of living—if only we allow ourselves to get close to it and to ponder on the relationship we all have with each other, other nations, cultures, and with the deeper meaning of life. As has been said by many sages, death puts life into perspective. And "God" (in whatever tradition) is love.

On Being Yourself

You must learn that you cannot be loved by all people.

You can be the finest apple in all the world—ripe, juicy, sweet, succulent, and offer yourself to all.

But you must remember that there will be people who do not like apples.

You must understand that if you are the world's finest apple, and someone you love does not like apples, you have a choice of becoming a banana.

But you must be warned that if you choose to become a banana, you will be a second-rate banana.

But you will always be the finest apple.

You must also realize that, if you choose to be a second-rate banana, there will be people who do not like bananas ...

Anonymous

CHAPTER NINE

Tools for Effective Communication

Good communication skills are the basis to forming a therapeutic partnership that brings satisfaction to the person receiving the care and to the person giving care. Good communication includes listening and observing. This includes body language and the tone of the voice as well as changes in the voice, which may indicate that something is being said that is not meant. After I established a good rapport, I was able to assess, observe, find out the person's preferences and choices, and begin the work of general advocacy and support.

I found that I needed to be sensitive to the timing of our communication. For example, if patients are vomiting and are uncomfortable, they will not feel like exploring spiritual concerns. If they are hungry or tired, they will need food or sleep before addressing issues of an intellectual nature. They may say or be feeling, "I'm too tired to think."

I needed to acknowledge that feelings belong to the patient or individual person and need not be taken personally. If I were to take personally the feelings that were being expressed, blocks in communication could easily develop. For example, if patients are angry because they are experiencing physical or emotional pain, and if they express that anger by verbally abusing me, I needed to recognize that the anger belonged to the patients and to the many sources of mental and emotional pain and confusion they may be experiencing.

I remember witnessing an occasion when a nurse responded

thoughtlessly to an angry patient by saying, "Don't talk to me like that." A kinder response could have been, "You may be angry, but I'm still here for you." There were times when feelings needed to be encouraged and I needed to give patients permission to be sad or angry. It is not helpful to jolly people out of their feelings without addressing the source of those feelings and giving them acknowledgement. I have distressing images in my mind of elderly people being jollied into playing a game of bingo or going on a bus trip. A more healing response may sound like this: "You sound as if you are very angry that your mother let your aunt bring you up as a child." "Is this the first time that you have had these feelings?" "I would feel angry, too, if I had been left in a wet bed for hours and no one came to answer my call bell." Just being listened to is empowering and gives a sense of self-worth. We don't always need answers.

I needed lots of practice in the area of listening, but I did have an appreciation for expressing feelings rather than letting them grow inside. This applied to those I cared for as well as those who were part of the caring team. Hand in hand with the expression of feelings is the need for forgiveness. Nothing new happens without forgiveness. Forgiveness is a choice. One option is to let go of the heavy feeling energy of hurt or grudge and to feel lighter and freer. Another option is to keep the heavy feeling energy within ourselves and to carry an emotional burden. There is a danger of repeating the same old karmic patterns, living with illusions and half-truths. There is an exchange of energy in any person-to-person interaction.

I looked for the patterns in people's behaviour from my understanding of the Myers Briggs Typology Indicator and appreciated the importance of the different needs of ethnic origin, culture, religion, social class, age, and occupation. There were times when I found that patients would repeatedly complain about their families and whether family members visited or did not visit and what they brought or didn't bring. I listened carefully to this talk while searching to find the root of the feelings of discontent. Listening is perhaps the most important gift we can all bring to care. Ultimately, a good listener paves the way for people to hear themselves. One way I would try to connect with a person was with the base energy chakra in mind. I would ask patients about their parents and how it was for them when they were growing up. My interest needed to be genuine because, at some level, it is easy to pick up on what is, or may be, fake.

In an end-of-life situation, if people can find value in their life experiences they will more easily find peace in their end-of-life experience. I would often ask people how they wished to be remembered as well as about the things they had done and accomplished and the things they had loved, such as places, people, music, ideas, sights, sounds, and interests. This took time, but gave results which would have been difficult to achieve with medications alone. A builder was proud of the fact that he could look across the city to the outline of buildings he had built. An Australian man was proud of the fact that he had invented the bobby pin, which held hair in place. Others made contributions in the worlds of art, fashion, business, and horse racing. My difficulty lay in finding a way to shine a light on the impermanence of all these achievements from a soul's perspective.

When it comes to communicating on a deeper level, much emotional pain stems from the family. The cause of the ongoing drama may be an inability to work through feelings of emptiness, abandonment, or the need for the unconditional love that comes from a parent. This is a practical application of holistic care in which the carer observes what is being expressed on an intellectual level and considers other causes. Hunger for the food traditionally served at the family table may cause the body to feel hungry as well as trigger a hunger for the emotional feelings sourced in family life. There is a common need for spiritual needs to be met. This is a time for sensitive listening as it is difficult to describe these needs. They be met by appreciating the beauty and perfume of fresh flowers and gazing at the wonder in a grandchild's eyes. Effective communication can be enhanced by an understanding of how and when we send and receive messages. These are a few tips I appreciated for breaking bad news:

- Deliver the bad news in a comfortable, quiet, and private place. Deliver it in person and with a supportive person present (if the patient desires) and with ample time allowed for reaction.

- Find out what the patient knows about his or her disease status and educate the patient as indicated.
- Determine how much the patient wants to know.
- Gently prepare the patient for bad news by using simple language and appropriate pauses to allow the patient to absorb the news.
- Empathize with the patient's emotions and be supportive of his or her feelings and concerns.
- Allow time for review, questions, and discussion.

At such sensitive and potentially difficult times, touch can be used to convey non-verbal communication. It is to be used thoughtfully to convey caring, but avoided if it is felt to be an intrusion of privacy. A hand placed on a shoulder can say a lot. One patient looked into my eyes and asked, "Am I dying?" I replied with a kiss placed on his brow. A nod of the head might have been another way of confirming what the patient already knew. Massaging a limb while talking to a patient is another way of communicating through touch. If I observed some swelling in a hand or ankle, I would ask if I could give the area a gentle massage. At times this became an opportunity to talk about painful memories. One man had very delicate thin skin from taking steroids over a long period. While I was dressing his legs, we communicated on many levels. Holding the hand of a person when he or she is very ill or frightened can be a simple means of offering comfort and non-verbally saying, "I'm here for you."

Where possible, I liked to use humour as a means of connecting soul to soul. This is not an easy tool to use and needs to come from a place of authentic trust. Members of the caring team would often be surprised to hear me talking to patients in a light-hearted way about serious conditions. I would warn them not to try to copy what I said but rather to use their own intuitive inner smile. Clown therapy is welcome in many healthcare settings—especially with children and in hospices. Laughter bubbles up from within like a natural spring—like tears. It is a giving of oneself. Kahlil Gibran, the poet and philosopher, wrote that joy is sorrow unmasked.

Communicating on spiritual issues is a sensitive area. Put simply, spirituality is the capacity to explore the inner self. The following are the words of Emeritus Professor Ian Maddocks AM. He has given me his permission to share them with readers.

> Throughout the world palliative care programs often started within a Christian community, and the Christian faith in the West has commonly underpinned palliative care and hospice initiatives. But in many societies, particularly those outside the Western tradition, Christians are a small minority, and the understandings of Islam, or the Buddha or of other religions need to be considered. Generalisations are clearly very difficult. But for many individuals' basic questions of identity and meaning: "Who am I?", "What meaning is there to my existence?", and "Is there significance in the way things are?" will arise in relation to this final part of life's journey. The term *spiritual* means different things to different people and is influenced by culture, religion, training and experience.

> In my consideration of spirituality I find a helpful term to use is *connectedness*. By experience we know ourselves and are known through our relationships and in the connection we make with our natural and human environment and with our own sense of self. When two persons "connect" with respect or love, something new, something greater than the sum of those two individuals may emerge. There is a magic in such connecting: it brings satisfaction, wonder, inspiration—a "spiritual" feeling. Such a feeling sometimes comes seemingly 'out of the blue'—undeserved, unheralded and an act of grace. This feeling may be felt also in beholding a superb view in nature, or the beauty of a small child at play, or a situation in which courage or patience or love is being demonstrated beyond expectation. From where

this feeling comes is a mystery; some name it as God, and purport to know it better; others recognize it as 'transcendent', breaking through from parts unknown; still others merely wait in simple wonder.

A sense of the spiritual is something commonly encountered in human crises that bring out the best of human qualities—resilience, patience, bravery, a willingness to sacrifice self. We connect with such examples, moved by them, aspiring to hope we too might demonstrate similar strengths if occasion demanded. It is a connectedness also commonly met in palliative care where we meet intimations of our own mortality. We need connectedness within ourselves also. We need to feel as far as possible complete, ready, open. We may seek to extend our connectedness with self through meditation, music or reading texts that give us energy and aliveness, and find it in the example and inspiration of another.

One of the topics of conversation I needed to be comfortable with was the near-death experience. Near-death experiences occur when people are on the brink of death—at times even believed to be clinically dead—yet somehow "return" to recount an intense spiritual experience. They often talk about going through a tunnel towards intense light and feeling a wondrous sense of peace. Following a near-death experience, some people experience a stirring of the soul and the need to live from a soul level. Cherie Sutherland, the author of *Transformed by the Light: Life after near-death experiences*, writes that life takes on a different face and there is a drastic change in priorities and a more developed sense of purpose following a near-death experience. The message from those who have survived a near-death experience is, "Death is all right. Don't be afraid. It's a beautiful place."

My own near-death experience occurred following a hysterectomy. I had haemorrhaged post-op and the foot of my bed had been raised. I remember feeling totally at peace knowing that my four children were all healthy and thriving and that I had tried to be a good wife and mother. What seemed to matter was that I had tried—there was no judgement. After an emergency procedure under general anaesthetic to stop the bleeding, I was surprised to find myself still alive and thought that I had better get on with living. I did not fear death again and, like many others who have had this experience, I was drawn to work with the frail elderly, dying, and with people who were grieving—drawing upon the lesson I'd learned all those years ago from my mummy cat who lost her kittens.

In aspiring to be midwives to the soul, we do well to be alive to the importance of other dimensions of consciousness and the different energy fields in a person's aura. The more we are comfortable with ourselves, in tune with our inner selves, and willing to risk connectedness with others, the better we are prepared to interact others. There is a need to be still and listen and to respond appropriately and intuitively rather than "by the book" or by some rule or precedent.

The degree of information to be given to the "unit of care" varies according to circumstances. Patients who have lived lives of taking responsibility for themselves may benefit from having their doctors tell them about the nature of their diseases, the treatments available, and the benefits—and possible burdens—of these treatments. Other people, who have different life experiences, may desire to know who will care for them. For some, bad news is a wake-up call and reminds them of the need to put their houses in order and deal with life issues that need completion. Some people will appreciate this wake-up call being delivered in a frank and pragmatic way, while others will appreciate the bad news delivered gently and over a period of time. However bad news is delivered, these points should always be considered:

- It is important that the process is begun at the time a life-threatening diagnosis is made.
- It is important to reassure patients with information about the support available by a palliative care team if needed.

- It is important to highlight what can be done to strengthen the spirit by removing despair even though curing the disease is not a realistic goal.
- It is important to remember that dying is a natural part of living and that, like living, dying benefits from education and preparation.

Our relationships with people often begin with bad news. People who receive such news can often remember to the minute when they received it. The messengers who bring bad news can also be irrationally blamed somehow for the news. Nurses and carers need to be aware of this and to offer to be the bearer of bad news in the place of a family member, for example. This way anger can be directed away from the family member. On one occasion, I was attempting to build rapport with a terminally ill patient and asked a question about her thoughts on her funeral. I received a barrage of "How dare you!" and the venting of much anger. This patient's husband, who had been present at the time, phoned me next day to thank me for being the catalyst for this release of emotion from his wife. He said he was pleased that it was directed at me, as he had the feeling that anything he did or said would be the trigger. This outburst opened up the channels of communication for all concerned.

For most doctors, it is important that they tell the truth and avoid lies and deceit that may cause distress at a later date. They do not want to enter into a "conspiracy of silence" as often requested by "well-meaning" relatives. There are gentle ways of telling the truth about something negative that can be a turning point in a person's known existence. This is a time for good clinical judgments and experience. This is also a time to be aware of the power of projections—when there is an unconscious and unacknowledged fear that is not recognized in the professional themselves, but rather mirrored onto the other person. "Know thyself" applies to all health professionals!

Sometimes what may be perceived as bad news can actually be good news for a patient. For example, Ella was in her eighties and had been diagnosed with cancer of the pancreas. She said that everyone seemed upset with the diagnosis, but she was rather relieved because she felt it was time to die.

The following story is adapted from *Chinese Idioms and Their Stories*:

> Long ago, there was a young man living in China. He had a mare, and one day the mare fled into an area ruled by tribes of minority nationalities. On learning this, his friends and relatives came to console him. However, his father told him; "Cheer up, son. Who says this may not be a blessing?"
>
> Several months later the mare returned with a group of fine horses. The friends and relatives came to congratulate the young man on his good fortune. The father, however said, "Who says this won't turn out to be a misfortune?"
>
> The young man loved his new horses, and every morning he took a ride on one of them. Since the new horses were not well tamed, the young man fell off one of them and broke his leg. On learning this, his friends and relatives came to console him. However, his father told him; "Cheer up, son. Who says this may not be a blessing?"
>
> A year later, the minority tribes began to invade into the area, and most young men were drafted into the army. As a cripple, the owner of the mare was not ordered to join the army, and he and his father survived the border war. "Therefore, a blessing may turn out to be a misfortune and the contrary may also be true," the story in the Writings of Prince Huainan concludes.

Let's take a look at ways we communicate:

- **Speaking**—This can be face-to-face or via the telephone. Much of the support given in palliative care is via the telephone. Doctors and nurses frequently carry paging devices and mobile phones, which give the reassurance that help is just a phone call away. Different tones of the voice communicate different messages.

- **Writing**—Sometimes writing things down is helpful, especially for medication instructions and appointments. Letters and information technology are effective and often help to clarify the question or problem. Cards are often used at anniversary (of death) times and for short acknowledgments.

- **Touch**—Touch is an effective non-verbal way of communicating. Holding a hand, stroking the hair, or wiping the brow with a cool cloth (perhaps with some aromatherapy such as lavender essence) are all ways of conveying care. A gentle massage may also communicate feelings of relaxation and care.

- **Facial expressions**—Smiles, frowns, and eye contact all convey messages. The degree of eye contact can sometimes depend on cultural differences.

- **Body language**—Frequently people use their hands to encourage or bring closure to conversation. People may turn their backs as a sign or stand with hands on hips in a show of authority. The way health professionals position themselves in relation to the patient or person is very important. For example, a person standing very upright with arms folded may not be perceived as being helpful. This body language is not conducive to effective communication with a person who is sitting or lying down. Body position and head movements can convey different messages.

- **Seeing**—Often diagrams and pictures can be effective communication tools, especially if the person is used to taking in information visually.

Here are some communication tips that can be useful for the caring team:

- Approach the person from the front if possible; otherwise, announce your arrival clearly and cheerfully. This will avoid frightening the person and will help to create a friendly atmosphere. Don't raise your voice unless you know that the person has a hearing impairment.

- Show warmth and interest by maintaining eye contact (unless culturally inappropriate) and a pleasant facial expression. A smile and kind eyes may be more effective than words. The way make-up is worn, and grooming can also give non-verbal messages.

- Introduce yourself and address the person by his or her preferred name. One day a nurse listened to a carer: "Put your feet together, dear. Now put your hands on the arms of the chair, dear. That's it, dear. Now, dear, do you want a cup of tea?" The nurse said to the patient, "Do you like being called dear?" "No, I do not!" was the patient's reply. Calling people by their names is a simple tool for helping them to feel validated. Ask if you are not sure—some people welcome being addressed by their given names, while others see this as disrespectful.

- Treat the person with respect. Talk *to* people not *at* people, and give them your full attention. Try to put aside thoughts of what you have just done or what you still have to do. "Now, Mrs, Jones, I want you to wear these stockings. They are needed for those swollen legs." This could be lightened by saying, "Hello, Mrs. Jones. Remember that I said I would look into getting you some stockings for those swollen legs?"

- Do not be afraid to touch the person. A handshake or friendly reassuring pat can open up conversation. Our own personal hygiene needs attention for close-up encounters, and strong perfume may not be appreciated.

- Speak slowly and clearly and be prepared to repeat things many times. Give the person time to pause and think and speak without interruption.

- Ask questions patiently and one at a time. By using open-ended questions, you give the person the opportunity to choose what he or she wants to say, as an open invitation has been given to the person to explore the issue further. For example, "I'd like to hear what you thought of the doctor's visit." "What did you do with the list of questions we made?" "What do we need to follow up?"

- Allow time for the person to respond, and while waiting, adopt body language that is relaxed and receptive. Sit in an "open" position. For example, don't stand over the person with your arms folded.

- Use short, simple familiar words: KISS = Keep it simple and succinct

- Use names when you refer to relatives or friends. Remember "the unit of care" is important in holistic care.

- Pay attention to the person's voice and gestures for clues of how he or she is feeling. Often people say things to please or according to what they think the carer wants to hear. They may deny pain, but grimace when they move.

- Do not ridicule the person if what he or she says sounds absurd. What may seem silly and trivial may mask another question, and people who are expected to know and understand may be reluctant to show their "ignorance." The principle of "informed consent" requires that explanations and alternatives must be given.

- Refrain from giving an opinion or offering advice.

- Seek clarification or help from an interpreter if you are unsure of the message being conveyed. Giving a summary of what is being said indicates that the message has been heard.

- Wait for a natural pause in the conversation before responding. So often when there is a flow of feelings, the flow is stopped by an interruption. This is especially so when tears are involved.

There are many levels of communication:

- **Cliché conversation**—This is made up of everyday greetings such as "How are you today?" "How nice to see you." These are superficial forms of chitchat. Responses come across as being more polite than accurate descriptions of feelings. Replies are conventional and automatic such as, "I'm fine, and how are you keeping?" There is very little depth to the conversation.

- **Reporting facts about others**—This level of conversation discusses another person or topic, but discloses very little of the person himself or herself. At this level of communication, people may talk about the weather, a news item, or the fact that someone known to both is in hospital.

- **Personal ideas and discernments**—This is a level of communication in which the speaker "tests the water" and a limited revelation about himself or herself occurs. If there is a sense of rejection or non-acceptance, the person will withdraw from giving ideas, decisions, and opinions. For example, a person may say that he or she does not believe in an afterlife. If this statement is received with a lack of respect for the opinion, and if an attempt is made to change or belittle the opinion, the person may not wish to see that person again.

- **Personal feelings**—Revealing feelings includes a level of risk-taking because our feelings are the core of our uniqueness. This is a deeper level of communication than only revealing ideas and judgements because a degree of trust is involved. That is why we say that a goal of the therapeutic relationship is trust. Sharing or disclosure at this level means that we can now begin to know others and ourselves.

- **Peak communication**—This is the level where absolute openness and honesty exists. It is the level of communication at which we are real. It requires trust, a non-judgemental attitude, acceptance, forgiveness, and unconditional love. At this level of communication, lasting friendships and marriages are made.

A bit of dialogue from a well-loved children's story gives us insight on being real. This dialogue, in *The Velveteen Rabbit* by Margery Williams, took place one day in a little boy's nursery between an old skin horse and a reasonably new velveteen rabbit. The skin horse had been the favourite plaything of the child's uncle, and had outlived many other nursery inhabitants of his generation. The rabbit was new to the nursery and felt the other more expensive toys snubbed him because they seemed to be so superior to him. The skin horse became aware of the rabbit's feelings and initiated this conversation:

> "What is *real*?" asked the Rabbit one day, when they were lying side by side near the nursery fender, before Nana came to tidy the room. "Does it mean having things that buzz inside you and a stick-out handle?"
>
> "Real isn't how you are made," said the Skin Horse. "It's a thing that happens to you. When a child loves you for a long, long time, not just to play with, but *really* loves you, then you become Real."
>
> "Does it hurt?" asked the Rabbit.
>
> "Sometimes," said the Skin Horse, for he was always truthful. "When you are Real you don't mind being hurt."
>
> "Does it happen all at once, like being wound up," he asked, "or bit by bit?"
>
> "It doesn't happen all at once," said the Skin Horse. "You become. It takes a long time. That's why it doesn't happen often to people who break easily, or have sharp edges, or who have to be carefully kept. Generally, by the time you are Real, most of your hair has been loved off, and your eyes drop out and you get loose in your

joints and very shabby. But these things don't matter at all, because once you are Real you can't be ugly, except to people who don't understand."

The Skin horse concludes his great philosophic speech with "but once you are Real you can't become unreal again. It lasts for always."

Source: Margery Williams—The Velveteen Rabbit

Internal dialogue affects the way others see us

Think about the way you talk to yourself. Do you put yourself down with thoughts that discount your abilities, or do you tell yourself that you can "do it"? Our conditioning may be attributed to parents who gave praise, rewards, or reproach when our actions were judged on their standards. Our peers may play a part: we may have been told not to be a "big head," and we may have had to play down our achievements.

We may feel unable to accept compliments, fearing that it would be immodest. How we communicate with ourselves is the basis for self-esteem. We also need to think about the way we treat others. Do we put them down and fail to give credit where credit is due? Often it is a poor self-image that looks for the negatives in others and criticizes them.

Using art as communication

Nancy Caldwell was the art therapist who came with me on an education visit to Sandakan Hospice, East Malaysia, in the year 2000. That year the theme was complementary therapies. Art plays a major role in hospice programs. She writes that art therapy is considered to be a communication, and in end-of-life situations can be useful for bringing clarity to what has been important to the person. As well as drawing and painting, scrapbooking and collage can be enjoyed, and they may be ways of retrieving hidden layers of memories. Modern technology means that copies of special photos, letters, and documents can also be included in the scrapbook or collage. I recall looking after one elderly lady who had a connection with Egypt and had many paintings, ceramic works of art, and wall hangings in her home from her time there. I photographed these reminders and printed them on my computer so that she could cut them out and paste them into a scrapbook that her carers were making with her guidance. They were indeed triggers for communicating feelings and current-day thoughts on past events and people. The activity was a happy one in spite of the fact that she struggled with dementia.

In recent times, I have facilitated soul collage sessions and wonder, as I cut out hundreds of images from magazines of all kinds, who will be drawn to a particular image. One image I remember well was that of a lone soldier standing in his uniform with a rifle on his shoulder. His face was lined with emotion. This image was chosen by a man who was, indeed, feeling lost and lonely and was evaluating the purpose of his life. In the process of preparing for these sessions I also am touched and "hear" the messages given to me by images or symbols. Children can benefit from being encouraged to draw about their happy and unhappy experiences. An art form I particularly enjoy is colouring in mandalas. *Mandala* is a Sanskrit word that means "circle." It represents wholeness, beginnings, and endings coming together and harmony. The mandala is a tool for insight meditation. The hand movements of colouring in occupy the conscious mind and, while being engaged in this activity, a person can access deeper levels of consciousness and be mindful of the colours they choose.

Using intuition as a communication tool

In general, the experience of "knowing" that comes with intuition brings a profound feeling of inner calm, certainty, and resolution. There can be a sense of rightness and appropriateness for saying what we say and expressing truth in our lives. It often requires courage to follow intuition.

Being sensitive to right timing is important, and it is said; "When in doubt, wait." Allowing time to observe whether an intuitive impression is validated by further inner and outer clues can often provide clarity. The mind offers a valuable tool to counterbalance and check intuitive insight. This has been likened to activities of the left side of brain, which values facts and details and is precise. This ability can help to clarify our insights and help us to communicate them. An intuitive message is often conveyed in symbols and metaphors that connect with feelings and thoughts. One proposal is that there is a realm of pre-existing ideas such as the "mind of God" or the "realm of ideas," as suggested by the ancient Greek philosopher, Plato, where this non-sensory information might originate.

Communication takes place on two levels, the subject level and the relationship level. If there is a good trusting relationship, people are able to agree or disagree without feeling uncomfortable or worthless. If this is not the case, every subject-level issue can become a test of the relationship; for example, when someone agrees with your views on an alternative therapy, religion, or philosophy, you could feel comfortable. However, when different views are shared, the relationship is tested unless founded on unconditional love, trust, and respect. Acceptance is different to agreement. Sometimes we are only accepted when we deal with facts and not feelings. If this is the case, the relationship is conditional.

People who are energized by outside factors	People who like to process internally
Communicate energy and enthusiasm	Keep their energy and enthusiasm inside
Respond quickly, without long pauses to think	Prefer to think before responding
Focus of their talk is on people and things in the external environment	Focus on internal ideas and thoughts
Need to moderate their expression	Need to be drawn out
Seek opportunities to communicate in groups	Seek opportunities to communicate one-to-one
Prefer face-to-face over written communication	Prefer written communication over face-to-face

Prefer to talk things out loud before coming to a conclusion	Prefer to come to a conclusion first before talking about it

People who are practical in orientation

People who make decisions from an irrational knowing

Prefer to have facts, details and examples presented first	Prefer to hear the broad issues presented first
Want practical and realistic applications shown	Want possible future challenges discussed
Rely upon direct experience to provide anecdotes	Rely upon insights and imagination to provoke discussion
Use an orderly step-by-step approach in presentations	Use a round-about approach in presentations
Prefer suggestions to be straightforward and feasible	Prefer suggestions to be novel and unusual
Are inclined to follow the agenda of a meeting	Are inclined to bypass the agenda
Refer to specific examples	Refer to general concepts

People who make head-based decisions:

People who make heart-based decisions:

Prefer to be brief and concise	Prefer to be sociable and friendly
Want the pros and cons of each alternative to be listed	Want to know the personal value of an alternative
Can be intellectually critical and objective	Can be interpersonally appreciative
Convinced by cool impersonal reasoning	Convinced by personal information enthusiastically delivered
Present goals and objectives first	Present points of agreement first
Consider emotions and feelings as data to weigh	Consider logic and objectivity as data to value
Seek involvement with tasks	Seek involvement with people

People who value being decisive may:	People who like to explore all options may:
Want to discuss schedules and timetables with tight deadlines	Be willing to discuss the schedule, but don't like tight deadlines
Dislike surprises, and prefer advance warning	Enjoy surprises, and like adapting to last minute changes
Expect others to follow through, and they count on it	Expect others to adapt to unexpected situations
State their position and decisions clearly	Present their views tentatively, and able to be modified
Communicate results and achievements	Communicate options and opportunities
Talk of purpose and action	Talk of autonomy and flexibility
Focus on the task to be done in a meeting	Focus on the process of a meeting

CHAPTER TEN

Making Friends with Loss, Grief, and Death

Perhaps the deepest reason why we are afraid of death is because we do not know who we are. We believe in a personal, unique, and separate identity—but if we dare to examine it, we find that this identity depends entirely on an endless collection of things to prop it up: our name, our "biography," our partners, family, home, job, friends, credit cards ... It is on their fragile and transient support that we rely for our security. So when they are all taken away, will we have any idea of who we really are?

—Sogyal Rinpoche, author of
The Tibetan Book of Living and Dying

Elisabeth Kübler-Ross called death "transition," and I feel that I am being led to continually "put my affairs in order." These preparations include seeing myself as a small ice block that melts into the one stream of consciousness that has no beginning and has no end. Be prepared! I recall a vivid dream I had in 1994. In this dream, I was standing on the edge of high cliff. At the bottom was the ocean, and behind me was a forest. Suddenly, out of the forest, and flying close to the ground, was a large aeroplane which I saw take a ninety-degree nose dive into the ocean. Then I observed the people in the plane, which was now horizontal, being welcomed and made happy! While I was puzzling over this, another plane came from the forest and flew straight on. I felt I was being given a choice. I could come home or fly on. Unconsciously I chose to fly on.

Rumi, the Sufi mystic and poet, wrote that the more awareness a person has, the deeper the soul. In the last phase of life, invariably we enter a time of reflection. A life is a story. I have listened to countless life stories—successful lives, inspiring lives, sad lives, tragic lives, fulfilled lives, and what may have been viewed as wasted lives. Whatever the life, there seems to be a deep need to tell, not only our story but also the stories of our ancestors. I found many indicators in the homes of patients that could initiate the telling of stories—photographs, paintings, a scar on a body, a wedding ring, a baked cake, a garden, a car, a pet, family members, war memorabilia, books. Stories can be told formally and informally, with relish and with shyness, with glee and with sorrow. I'm learning about sharing stories with a group of women who meet regularly to colour in mandalas. Carol Omer has published a book called *Big Girls Little Colouring Book: Healing Mandalas for Relaxation and Stress Relief* and is the leader of this group. She writes that *mandala* is the Sanskrit word for "circle," and in this world of complexities, returning to the circle, which mirrors the womb of creation, is an open-eyed meditation. It is an illusion to think in the conscious or waking mind that today's perceptions are somehow wiser than those of previous generations. There is an undercurrent of timeless wisdom to be sourced in the different levels of consciousness.

Apart from the theory on grief, I have been privileged to observe how people without theoretical knowledge deal with grief. Princess Diana's death touched people in ways that hadn't before been imagined. All those flowers! She was indeed a flower princess who overcame much pain and misunderstanding. I once looked after an Irish man who loved to play golf. His cancer had left him with wounds to his abdomen that would not heal. He just wanted to be taken home to die. This we did. At five o'clock his friends came for a visit and to share a traditional beer. All he could manage in his weakened state was to suck his beer from a jumbo cotton wool swab. It didn't stop his friends from raising their glasses in a supportive and honouring way. After his death, his neighbours from a European background arrived on the doorstep with a tray carrying a fresh pot of coffee and some freshly baked scones. The man carrying the tray said that this was their tradition and way of supporting a grieving household. When I was preparing the man's body, his wife had me dress him in the clothes he wore to golf—including a bright green pullover. She kept him at home for twenty-four hours before letting the funeral people take him.

It is common for a grieving person to be avoided because many people do not know what to say by way of offering comfort. Rather than avoidance, which isolates the grieving person, it is far better to say, "I know you are hurting, and I wish there was something I could do or say to comfort you." When words fail, a hug or a casserole can speak volumes. Be present and just listen. With regard to casseroles, one elderly gentleman whose wife had recently died told me that he had been warned about women bearing casseroles by the men in his club—these women may have an ulterior motive. It is a time when vulnerability may cloud judgement. Men and women grieve differently. Women are better, it seems, at sharing feelings. Men, it would seem, may need a sexual connection to express feelings and can be very vulnerable in a time of grieving. This was the case for a father of two teenage children. Within a very short time after the death of his wife, he began a relationship with another woman. The children rightly felt that they had lost two parents.

One theory I found to be helpful in my understanding of grief was Granger Westberg's model, which he describes in his book, *Good Grief*:

- **Shock**—A state of "temporary anaesthesia" which helps grievers maintain a calm aspect in the early stages of grief. The person seems unable to take in the reality, to move or make decisions.
- **Emotional release**—Pent up feelings are released and may be expressed by weeping, stamping the feet, shouting, etc. The person may idealize the loss in an attempt to come to terms with the

emotions they he or she is feeling. The release may represent the grief of former losses.

- **Depression and isolation**—This is a time of acute despair and loneliness when it seems that the sun never shines and black clouds dominate and the future is grey and endless. The person withdraws from life and may be overwhelmed with self-pity. Viktor Frankl, the founder of logotherapy, taught that despair was suffering without meaning.

- **Physical symptoms**—These may include loss of appetite, weight loss, inability to sleep or concentrate, headaches, various aches and pains, and acute anxiety. They may include the symptoms experienced by the person who has died.

- **Panic**—There may be a terrifying feeling of losing one's mind. Irrational thoughts, fears, and feelings that are usually controlled run riot. There may be a preoccupation with the loss and there may be disorganization. The person may have a sense of the presence of, or "see," the deceased.

- **Guilt**—This may be out of proportion with the reality of the situation. There may have been regretful last words or treatments not tried.

- **Hostility and resentment**—It is common for a person to seek to blame when things go wrong. Frequently blame is directed at other people including the health professionals. Even when the person knows that there is no blame, hostile feelings are present.

- **Inability to return to normal activity**—This may be out of a fear of losing control of emotions or feeling that a sad person is not welcome to return to previous activities. This is especially so in a society that tends to deny death as a normal part of life and so doesn't know what to say to a grieving person. There may be a lack of energy to make an effort.

- **Re-emergence of hope**—The deepest darkest grief begins to lessen, and an interest in life re-emerges. This point may be one of conflict because the person feels a loyalty towards the past and a natural urge to return to life and the living: the present feelings seem unreal.

- **Readjustment to reality**—This is the final of Westberg's stages. A new and different horizon arises, and energy is renewed. How quickly this happens may depend on the character of the person and the coping skills he or she has developed during his or her lifetime. It is a tribute to the human spirit that people can work through grief and emerge even stronger. In this period, it is important to keep activities simple and manageable. It is a time to avoid confronting situations. Above all, it is a time to let go of events and people in life that no longer serve a positive outcome. It is a time to go forward without survivor guilt and anger over a life situation and to do this without useless blame.

Again, there is no one right way to grieve, but there are pitfalls to be avoided. Emotions are not necessarily rational, and it is best to avoid making decisions in the early stages of grief. I have lived on my own since my divorce in 1992 and was comforted by books from the author Robert Johnson who discusses the psychology of love as a cultural phenomenon in the West. He describes the quest for romantic love as our obsession, our pathology, our replacement for religion in a secular age. In my own life, I have been striving to understand the psychology of romantic love—the anima and animus as described by Jung. I have intended to combine these feminine and masculine energies within my own psyche rather than to see them in another and perhaps fall in love with what I am seeing. Perhaps, instead of a marriage between two people, I fell in love with my work, or perhaps I do not have the archetype of a wife. I know I have the archetype of a mother and a healer.

I felt my grief as a heaviness in my very being. A common way of dealing with grief is to become busy. Busy I was. Then there was the added trauma of surviving the first three months in Malaysia. It seemed that my way of dealing with the grief of divorce was to give myself a course in how to survive in a foreign land. My drive was to contribute to the cause of spreading the hospice philosophy and palliative care. I embraced this new discipline in medicine and its potential to improve end-of-life care. I experienced further losses upon my return home from Malaysia. Two women were living with me who were on the Rotary matching grant program. One evening I had taken them to a performance by the Australian ballet. On returning home, I found the front door to be unlocked. Strange. Then, when I felt for the light switch, there was no light. The power had been switched off, which meant that the alarm had not sounded. I had been robbed of money and jewellery. Much of the jewellery had been part of my former life as the wife of an orthodontist. Instead of replacing the jewellery, I chose to accept money from the insurance company for a new carpet in the office. Fortunately, I was wearing the one piece of jewellery I value to this day. It is a ring made from my mother's wedding ring, two small diamonds from her engagement ring, and a larger diamond given to me by the father of my children.

Grief is too often associated with the death of a physical body. There is much we can learn from grief. In the case of my burglary, I had the opportunity to examine what I really valued. When my father died, I was the mother of two young children. One was born in England and the other was born in Rochester, New York. When I came home to Australia, we lived in another state from our families, and I had two other children without help from family members, who lived thousands of miles away. My grief was put on hold because I needed to give my attention to my children and my husband, who was at the time, a university lecturer. Years later, when he began a private orthodontic practice, I was needed to entertain potential sources of referral and to be involved in the wider dental community.

When I lived in London, I had attended several courses at the famous Cordon Bleu school of cooking in Marylebone Lane, London. I took my course with young girls who were debutantes who talked about their coming-out dances and parties. I was paired with a man who was a butler. He asked me if I was in service too, and my haughty pride replied, "No! I'm a registered nurse." The second course was with women who were going into their own kitchens for the first time. They could no longer employ a cook, and their conversations centred on what picnic baskets they would take to the famous Ascot horse race. For those women, the circumstances of a change in position and having to learn new work was experienced with all the feelings associated with loss. This particular course included flower arranging, which I particularly enjoyed, and it taught me ways to bring my family home garden indoors.

Our family home was built on the slope of a hill, so much of the garden was terraced. It was largely planted with flowering native bushes and fruit-bearing trees. The children derived much enjoyment from the many games they were able to play on the lawn tennis court with its high fence. The tennis court was also the site for birthday party games, and where I celebrated my fiftieth birthday together with my daughter who was celebrating her twenty-first. The theme for this party, which was held in a marquee, was Hawaiian. Another notable party was held for one of my sons and his friend to mark their eighteenth birthdays. It was a reverse-attire party where the boys wore dresses, wigs, and high heels, and the girls wore dinner suits. I mention this to highlight the grief associated with the breakup of a family unit. Another loss I experienced was the loss of faith in traditional religion.

Prior to my marriage, I became a member of the Catholic Church. Along with catechisms which sum up the beliefs of the Catholic faithful and authoritative statements by the Pope, this little girl, who grew up close to nature and was raised by parents who read inspiring verse each morning after breakfast, found much to question. In my initial instruction, I remember asking many questions and being told by the priest that, if I wanted to join a club, I needed to accept the rules of the club. In my view, there were many rules in the Catholic religion to be questioned. These rules I tried to obey for nearly forty years until my quietly prodding inner voice led me to believe that I didn't need to be a member of the Catholic Church (or any other religion) to live a meaningful life of service and calling.

When I first became a Catholic, there was much I appreciated about this large family of faithful. Yet, I missed the hymn singing and uplifting energy that I had experienced in the Methodist church. When I became a Catholic, the Mass was in Latin and one of the rules that inconvenienced my friends was not being able to eat meat on Fridays. This changed following the Second Vatican Council. While there was no need to wear Sunday best clothes, it was a struggle getting four young children to Mass each Sunday and answering their frequent question: "Why do we have to go?" I did appreciate many of the Church sacraments—especially I valued receiving a pre-birth blessing and can see the value in the sacrament of Confession when it comes to healing the soul. Florence Nightingale also questioned the religions of her time and wrote that she prized freedom of thought and saw it as a privilege for oneself and something to respect in others. She questioned that the "word" could be pinned down to either one period or to one church. Today I question the virgin birth but appreciate the divine feminine archetype that Mother Mary represents. I feel humbled by the beauty and the tragedy of the Jesus and Mary story.

My time in Greece with Jean Houston in 2014 and 2015 gave me a new way of appreciating the god and goddess archetypes and how a person can relate to the messages and teachings that they convey. I learned that the goddess Demeter was the fertility goddess and embodied the highest mysteries of human nature. Her work is seen in the change of seasons which also represent the ebb and flow of a person's emotional and spiritual life. Aphrodite was the great Olympian goddess of beauty, love, pleasure, and procreation and is said to be able to bring about the transformation of humans through the enigmas of beauty and love. Aries was the great Olympian god of war, battle-lust, civil order, and manly courage. Asclepius was the god of medicine who taught that the cause of illness lay in the psyche and that it manifested both physically and spiritually. These are just a few examples of the characteristics of the ancient Greek gods and goddesses. The Greek people used tragedies, myths, and symbols to give birth to philosophy and deep questioning. In the ancient Greek amphitheatres, the people of the day saw their unconscious personal dramas played out in front of them. This period of history was a rich tapestry which depicted the choices people have in the way they live their lives and the grief that may follow unwise choices. Today's sporting and pop star heroes seem to be less helpful in inspiring the choices I make.

Viktor Frankl, the professor of neurology and psychiatry at the University of Vienna Medical School, spent three years during World War II in concentration camps. His psychotherapeutic school is founded on the belief that striving to find meaning in life is the most powerful motivation for human beings. He taught that despair is suffering without meaning. Grief is suffering. Our task is to find meaning and to still continue to live and grow. On a visit to South Africa, I experienced the heavy energy of grief—it was everywhere. I saw it in the eyes of the porter at the game park I visited. I saw it while driving along the garden route where the ocean and expensive houses were on one side of the bus and the miles and miles of poor makeshift shelters were on the other side of the bus. My heart felt heavy while listening to the stories of those who lived through the separation forced on black and white people. More shocking was to hear that the reason for apartheid was preached from the pulpits of churches. Such suffering. Even in a community hospice in 2007 the black and white people had to attend the day hospice program on different days.

I often reflect on a lesson or guidance received on the snow fields. This was a family skiing holiday, and at previous ski holidays, I had joined the children in a beginner's class. Of course, with their agile and fit bodies, they progressed faster than I could and were soon all over the mountain. The next year, I had a private instructor and loved the one-to-one attention. Then my husband reminded me that a class was cheaper than private tuition. He kindly said that he would join me in a class, and I appreciated this offer. The ski instructor had the class begin at the top of a slope and ski down towards him. We were divided into his left and right side. My husband and I were on two different sides. When my husband asked if he could join me, the instructor replied, "Oh, sir, your wife is better than you are, and I wouldn't want you to hold her back!" Later I heard these words from a clairvoyant: "He is a good man, but he held you back." I tell these stories as examples of loss for both of us. He was losing the wife of his dreams and his template of a husband's role, and I was being drawn into a future of fulfilment in a trial by fire. The spiritual writer, Eckhart Tolle, talks about the ego needs. We had both been living largely from ego needs. Loss of ego is commonly understood but maybe not thought of in the context of loss and grief. "I don't know who I am anymore."

Grief is emotional pain energy and is frequently stored in the body.

I mentioned earlier that emotions are felt in the body but feelings are understood in the mind. I have experienced times during a massage when sorrow in some form arose. Skin hungers for touch in some people whose energy is heavy with grief. Other people I know who have experienced deep grief cannot bear to be touched—they seem to be fearful of letting open the floodgates of sorrow. Because grief is hidden in the unconscious, it is difficult to recognize and so work on. Grief is difficult work. People who have experienced loss need to understand that their feelings are valid, that there are no right or wrong feelings. Feelings simply are. We cannot invent a feeling; it just happens or arises. Expression in some way, oral or written, facilitates release. Feelings are uniquely personal. I have found the most helpful therapists to be ones who can delve into the past with techniques such as life alignment and hypnosis. Life alignment is a natural therapy that addresses all areas of one's life and taps into the unconscious. It uses applied kinesiology and pendulum dowsing to identify the root causes of pain, illness, and "stuckness."

"Tears are the sprinkler system of the soul." I learned this saying from a friend who is a nun. The more grieving people cry, the more they water their souls and grow. People grieve at different levels and at different times. Loss includes the loss of dreams. One cannot make an appointment with grief. It just happens. Events, human interaction, music, and art have the potential to trigger feelings and emotions in a person. Grief, like death, can put life into perspective. At first grief confronts us with a number of unpleasant discoveries. Many things are changing. The spouse who faithfully visited the nursing home each day to feed a partner will not know what to do when the person dies. There is a loss of purpose in one's day. Grief is experienced. A person with dementia will forget that the person he or she visited in the nursing home has died, and will want to visit anyway. The feelings of connectedness remain. There is no end to grief.

There is so much grief connected to the many different types of dementia. When the frontal lobe is affected, a person may need help to begin a simple task such as eating or dressing. While such people may face many losses, being in nature and especially in their own gardens, seems to bring comfort. Pets can be a comfort. There is also an experience of loss for those who are responsible for their care. Without being able to obtain facts such as a description of how the person slept and what he or she needed or why he or she was calling out, the carer is left with an empty and unsatisfied feeling of loss. In grief counselling I would often use a visualization based on visiting a garden in the mind's eye as I sat by the chair or bedside. One night I chose to describe a rose garden to a patient only to learn the next morning when a son came to visit that, indeed, roses were his mother's favourite flower. When the conscious mind fails, the unconscious mind of the senses still seems to operate. Successful or not, my intention was focused on being a source of light and love.

In my own life, I still feel the loss caused by a divided family. Over the years, as my children married, had children of their own, and experienced their own emotional distresses, there were moments of heaviness in my body. We are all connected. While their father and I shared the rituals of weddings, christenings, and family celebrations, I was sensitive to the presence of sadness and grief. The rational mind reminded me that I could not have had my freedom and the experiences as a soul mid-wife if I had remained a marriage partner. I found comfort when reflecting on how a pearl is formed: from constant irritation, the mollusc repeatedly secretes a substance to cover the irritant which becomes a valuable beautiful gem. Layers of life experiences covered my irritant small self, transforming it to a smoother, more glowing, and more rounded small self.

Grief has many faces and may leave emotional scars.

- It is important to understand that there is no end-point to grief and that a death in present time may be an unexpected reminder of a past loss. This may trigger another pang of grief accompanied by vivid memories. The stories we cling to are stored in our nervous system and unconscious mind. They, like recurring dreams, need to be resolved.
- The pain of yearning may diminish with time, talk, and tears, and the good memories may surface to be enjoyed. Age, gender,

circumstances, and world philosophy all affect the normal grieving process; however, there will always be a bond in the deeper layers of consciousness.

- It is important not to stereotype people or to expect them to go through the commonly described stages in a linear fashion.
- It is important to remember the special days such as birthdays, anniversaries, and religious festivals. It is at these times that the pain of loss returns. Some writers say that four months after a death is an important time. At that time, the grieving person begins to grieve for the person whom the deceased *represented*— for example, the husband and protector—rather than to grieve for the person who was suffering and dying from cancer. It is also a time when friends and neighbours, who gave tender loving care following the loss, may feel that they are no longer needed, and return to their own affairs. Another example of complicated grief is the idolization of the deceased person that sometimes occurs during the stages of grief. In this instance, people grieve for the "wished for" person.
- Grief heals in its own time. I remember a Californian nurse healer sharing her method of managing grief. She would make a cut on the trunk of a tree in her garden and watch it heal as she was healing.

The most beautiful people we have known are those who have known defeat, known suffering, known struggle, known loss, and found their way out of the depths. These persons have an appreciation, a sensitivity, and an understanding of life which fills them with compassion, gentleness, and a deep loving concern. Beautiful people do not just happen.

—Elisabeth Kübler-Ross

Some people may hold the belief that wounds deserve to be rewarded if there is a just God. There are times when people hold onto a "poor me" attitude because it gains welcome attention from other people. In my own life, I strive to practise self-responsibility and to look for lessons and guidance. I have been guilty of defining myself by what I was—the palliative care nurse and counsellor. There were times that I would have been pleased to have been acknowledged for my work by my peers. I have a calling to pass on the knowledge that I have gained at the bedside of people at the end of their lives. Today, I can see how limiting that acknowledgement would have been if I had followed the traditional medical model. My life can be likened to the butterfly. It experiences a transformation process before the final struggle to escape from the cocoon and to fly free. The butterfly reminds me that there is another way to look at the losses I experienced—they had the potential to transform me from seeking worldly success to having an appreciation of a deeper mode of existence.

In *The Book of Joy: Lasting Happiness in a Changing World*, by Dalai Lama, Desmond Tutu, and Douglas Abrams, conversations between His Holiness the Dalai Lama and Archbishop Desmond Tutu are recorded. The message given by the Dalai Lama on death is that life is short and it is important to make life meaningful while we are alive. There is a profound teaching by an ancient Tibetan Master:

> The true measure of spiritual development is how one confronts one's own mortality. The best way is when one is able to approach death with joy; next best way is without fear; third best way is at least not to have regrets.

I say that I am not afraid of death and believe that we are empowered or imprisoned by how we look at death. I have an outer self or form and conscious perception. I have an inner self of dreaming, imagination, and creativity that links to vast consciousness. I have a higher self or soul that continues from lifetime to lifetime adopting different personalities. Pain and suffering come with attachment—attachment to the emotional body and life's dramas and to the egoic mind which needs to be right and to divide into right and wrong, black and white, godly and ungodly, light and dark. Beyond the egoic mind, these illusions disappear. However my life has evolved, I have no sense of blame when I say, "I did it my way."

> When I die my deeds will follow along with me—that is how I imagine it. I will bring with me what I have done. In the meantime it is important to ensure that I do not stand at the end with empty hands.
>
> —Carl G. Jung

AFTERWORD

The end of my nursing career came as a shock. I knew that I could not continue with administration responsibilities and patient care. I was, after all, seventy-eight years old. The surpluses from the nurse practice funded the education and community awareness programs that were run by the not-for-profit NurseLink Foundation. Along came an offer from a nurse who wanted to take over the nurse practice, which was well on the way to being reaccredited. However, it was this nurse's intention to run the practice as a for-profit enterprise. That left the foundation's administration, education programs, and the quarterly newsletter, "Heart and Soul," without a regular income stream. Within a short time, the foundation, which had always been a public not-for-profit company with charitable status, went into voluntary closure.

I knew I needed help and that it was time for my responsibilities to diminish. I envisioned myself as continuing to edit "Heart and Soul" and being a volunteer counsellor and educator. This was not to be. Following the sale of the nurse practice, which had happened during a time when I was in another state, I visited the office with a welcoming bouquet of flowers and a thoughtfully worded card. There was an awkward silence, and I was told very politely that I was not wanted in the practice or in the foundation—even as a volunteer. I was stunned. Even with the ending of my marriage I'd had some warning signs of change. In retrospect, this sudden death was a blessing in disguise. There was a change of name and in how nursing was conducted. The personal approach to care that I had fostered had been replaced with technology. Spirituality cannot be taught. It is discovered by experience. It is experienced through relationship with self, others, and the indefinable nature of soul.

I will share with you a profound spiritual experience I had at Cape Sounion in Greece on the final day of my time with Jean Houston in 2014. We had climbed the hill to the site of Poseidon's temple. Poseidon was the god of the oceans and horses. He personified the instinct that drives change and drives a person to wander through endless adventures, only to return to the place where the journey started and to see it again anew. He represented the god of earthquakes and the unconscious, both beauty and terror. As a group, we were sitting and standing near Jean and listening to her wisdom. I was wearing a white poncho and standing with arms outstretched when I felt, in no uncertain terms, the breath of Poseidon fill my sails! I felt not only renewed with energy, but also that I would have assistance on my journey—wherever my sails took me. Next morning, before breakfast, I entered the waters of the Aegean Sea and sunk below the surface of the water three times as a symbol of baptism into the next phase of my life.

At the time of my divorce, a grief counsellor who worked for my practice said, "Joy, God removes from your life that which is no longer useful." Unlike Florence Nightingale, I had experienced the birth of children and a married life that she had railed against, saying that a married woman did not exist in the eyes of the law, and if she was to follow her own interests, these had to be at odd moments—creative work requires the whole of one's time! My soul was under contract, it seemed then, and is so today as I continue to grow and learn to meld more deeply into the mysterious. For too long I defined my life by what I did rather than who I am. I have been known to say that dying is like going into a darkened room and searching for the light switch. There can be a moment of fear that is quickly overshadowed with expectation and the excitement of coming home.

Today I coordinate Soul Talks for the benefit of those people who live in Adelaide and also for those who connect via recordings on the website soultalks.com.au. This monthly program gives voice to health professionals who bring a deeper perspective to their work. The soul's journey in a lifetime is about healing in all aspects of the personality—physical, emotional, and mental. The soul does not die. The soul is much more than the physical body. It is in the physical form not merely to obey rules and dogma but rather to be a creative, alive, and growing force. Consciousness is not lost when the body dies. A spiritual practice which surrenders to the higher intelligence is not a function of the ego. A spiritual practice can enable a soul to melt into the vastness of what is beyond what my small mind can comprehend.

When dying a person is in the presence of truth.
—Sogyal Rinpoche

ACKNOWLEDGEMENTS

Firstly, I would like to acknowledge my spiritual guides—seen and unseen. Chief among these is Florence Nightingale. These guides were beside me in my service to the greater good as a private palliative care nurse. Secondly, I would like to acknowledge the wisdom and insights I have gained from webinars and, in some instances, personal contact with: Jean Houston, Peggy Rubin, Caroline Myss, Andrew Harvey, Mirabai Starr, Father Richard Rohr, Eckhart Tolle, and Thomas Huble. These modern mystics encouraged me to search the world within for universal truths and to build a bridge from past experiences and expressions to the present.

I would like to thank Emeritus Professor of Palliative Care Ian Maddocks AM who took a risk in supporting my work when I did not seem to fit in with traditional hospice ways. I wish to thank him and Professor David Currow for sharing their palliative medicine knowledge in the education courses I coordinated in Australia and Malaysia. While many people contributed to the Sandakan Hospice programs in East Malaysia, Peter Roberts, who plays the harp to those who are dying, will not be forgotten. I am proud to be a patron of this hospice. Invitations for this rich international sharing came from my good friend and dynamic nurse, Margaret Lieu.

Closer to home I wish to acknowledge the support I received from friends and family members who may have been seeking a more traditional wife, mother, grandmother, and friend. I was extremely proud to have my three sons serve on the NurseLink Foundation board. All my children, while students, worked with patients and, at times, in the office. My eldest son, Michael, is a much-respected GP in a large country town; additionally he works for the aboriginal community. His sister, Susan, practises as an integrative GP and commits herself to partnering with patients to achieve the freedom of mind and body that comes from recovery and rejuvenation. She also offers health and wellness events at Bird in Hand winery. My third child, Justin, has a business degree in marketing as well as a law degree. His positive energy is spread widely. As well as being a global ambassador for Bird in Hand winery, he uses his creativity in other global networks. My youngest son, Andrew, is the executive director of the world-class Bird in Hand winery in the Adelaide Hills. The Bird in Hand Foundation today supports my Soul Talks program as well as giving back to the community by helping the young, the underprivileged, or those who just need that little extra helping hand.

Each of my four children has three children. It is such a pleasure to watch them grow up and achieve their potentials.

No words can express the gratitude I feel for the patrons of NurseLink Foundation and the directors of the NurseLink Foundation Board who shared their lifetime skills and knowledge to support my vision.

Louise Hay's book, *You Can Heal Your Life*, was in my library soon after I began my practice and taught me to seek ways to heal myself— rather than to outsource my ills to others.

I am appreciative of my friendship with Rita Ward who directed Elisabeth Kübler Ross's work in Australia. She taught me to have courage and to explore my own path. I am also appreciative of good friends, Nancy Caldwell, Lyn Rose, and Dr. Margaret Sullivan who skilfully read the manuscript and reported on punctuation and lack of clarity.

Then there is my graphic designer, Frank Stillitano, who first came to me as a student of his craft. Today he manages my website and understands what I want when the right words cannot express what is in my mind.

Named or unnamed, I send love and gratitude.

GLOSSARY

Archetypes

Archetypes are patterns of psychological energy that provide effective frameworks for self-awareness. They are found in the collective unconscious and are commonly recognized universal symbols. They include the mother, the child, the victim, the healer, the saboteur, the warrior, the wise old man, the teacher, the nurse, the seeker, the rebel, the queen, and more. As well as having virtues, they also have shadow sides. For example, the shadow side of the queen may be recognized when the person is controlling and demanding rather than being a benevolent authority. The ancients understood the world to be the product of five archetypical forces: ether, air, fire, water, and earth. The characteristics of star signs can be understood as archetypes.

Aura

The aura is a radiant energy field that surrounds the body and permeates it. It is made visible by Kirlian photography. It has been described as an ovoid rainbow-tinted cloud of light. When consciousness departs at death, the aura withdraws. Dora Kunz, who is the co-founder of Therapeutic Touch, writes, "The aura is a representation of our innate character, an indication of our potentials and a record of our experiences."

Chakras

The chakras are spinning wheels of energy or organs of consciousness and energy within the personal aura. They can be used as a road map to gaining an understanding of the world of energy. There are seven major centres which energize and control the body and its inner organs. Blockages in the flow of energy can adversely affect the body and organs. They are activated by concentrated thought. The chakras are located at the crown of the head, brow, throat, heart, solar plexus, genital region, and base of the spine. The psychological foundation of the chakras has its roots in Hinduism.

Dark Night of the Soul

This is the name of a poem written by sixteenth century Spanish Christian Mystic, St. John of the Cross. It is a term used to describe the experience of a dark mood and the loss of a perceived meaning and purpose in life. It can be viewed as an experience of detaching from what was formerly believed in order to gain a deeper perception of the "one consciousness." Sufi wisdom may describe it as a crushing of the grapes to make wine, which is the fruit's real essence, and an opening up to the universal field, which reorganizes.

Energy Medicine

Energy medicine is a broad range of approaches for healing that centre around the human energy system, including the science of intuition. It considers that energy originating in the mind manifests in the body. The foundation of energy medicine in healthcare is the belief that everything that exists—everything that we see, sense, or feel—is energy. Beyond the surface of our awareness lies the vast vibration of energy. A physical body is comprised of various energy fields and energy systems. There are fields of emotional energy and mental energy arising from thought patterns and experiences. Energy does not differentiate between physical and emotional problems. Caroline Myss says this about energy medicine:

According to energy medicine we are all living history books. Our bodies contain our history—every chapter, line and verse of every event and relationship in our lives. As our lives unfold, our biological health becomes a living, breathing biological statement that conveys our strengths, weaknesses, hopes and fears.

Enneagram

The Enneagram is a powerful approach to understanding the psychology, emotions and behaviour of ourselves and others. It describes the gifts and the challenges of each personality style and has its origins in ancient wisdom traditions. It is designed to help people pay attention to their primary drives, passions, and compulsions with the use of a circular diagram. Around the diagram at the points of three enclosed triangles there are nine numbers, which symbolize different personality styles. These numbers are divided into three centres. The triad of the numbers two, three, and four represents a feeling centre; the triad of five, six, and seven represents a thinking centre; and the triad of eight, nine, and one represents an instinctual centre. The Enneagram represents interconnectedness and gives seekers insight and understanding into their deeper layers of soul.

Karma

Karma is the result of the choices a person makes. Eastern philosophies describe karma as the sum of a person's actions in this and previous lifetimes and the universal law of cause and effect. The intention behind each action influences karma. Esoteric philosophy teaches that the soul is always subject to the karmic actions of the personality. The personality, in energetic terms, is made up of a physical body, an emotional body and a mental body.

Life Force

Life force is what animates. It permeates all living things. The

Chinese call it *chi*. The Japanese call it *ki*, and the Indian yogis call it *prana*. Love, which is a vibratory force, is the core essence of the life force. The life force and the healing process work with complexity and wisdom. The basic premise is that energy follows thought. Laughter, the honest expression of feelings, and the impact of tender loving care and touch all enhance the life force.

Myers Briggs Typology Indicator (MBTI)

The MBTI is a well-researched, introspective, self-reporting questionnaire inventory for learning one's preferred way of living in the world and how to understand and appreciate differences among other people. The work is based on C. G. Jung's observation of personality types and aims to aid people in appreciating that differences in personality have the potential to complement the workings of an organization and of relationships.

Reiki

The word means "universal life energy," and the therapy is a form of spiritual practice which channels this universal life energy via the hands. The Reiki symbols were shown to Dr. Usui, who was a learned Japanese man. In his search for truth, he meditated and fasted on the Holy Mountain of Kuriyama where, in a great white light, he saw the ancient Sanskrit Reiki symbols glowing in shining gold. They are passed on to healers via attunements from a Reiki master. For true results, Dr. Usui discovered that the person receiving Reiki must to be willing to receive the energy.

Shadow

Jung's description of the shadow can include everything outside the light of consciousness, and may be positive or negative. Shadow work is about bringing to light the darkness or shadows of our lives and healing them. These include the influences of collective trauma as seen in the treatment of some women and war situations. The shadow influences every part of a person's life. It isn't bad and may hold unrealized potential. It is found in the stories that a person clings to and in archetypical patterns. Since it's hidden from awareness, it is difficult to control and can become compulsive. Once it is brought into the light of awareness, it no longer has power over a person.

Unconditional Love

This is the kind of love that asks for nothing in return. Dr. Elisabeth Kübler-Ross recommended that it be given with a non-judgemental attitude. She wrote that we discover our true identities and greatness by letting go of all the illusions of identity and that love is the source of truth. It is love that exists because of who we are rather than what we do or do not do. Love is a universal vibration and loving hands are healing hands.

BOOKS THAT HAVE INFLUENCED MY WORK

Ajemian, Ina, and Balfour M. Mount. 1982. *The R.V.H. manual on palliative/hospice care*. Salem, New Hampshire: The Ayer Co.

Alexander, Eben. 2013. *Proof of Heaven*. New York: Simon and Schuster.

Armstrong, Karen. 1993. *A History of God*. Great Britain: William Heinnemann Ltd.

Augsberger, David. 1981 *Caring Enough to Forgive*. California: Regal Books.

Baginski, Bodo, J. 1988 *Reiki—Universal Life Energy*. USA: Life Rhythm.

Barbato, Michael. 2009 *Reflections on a Setting Sun*. Australia: Griffin Press.

Bowker, John. 1993. Canto Edition. *The meaning of death*. UK: Cambridge Uni. Press.

Burdman, Geri Marr. 2008 *Search for Significance—Finding Meaning in Times of Change, Challenge and Chaos*. US: Bellevue Press.

Calabria, Michael D, and Janet A. Macrae. 1994. *Suggestions for thought by Florence Nightingale*. Philadelphia: University of Pennsylvania.

Ciyun, Zhang, 1996. *Chinese Idioms and their Stories.* Beijing: Foreign Languages Press.

Chodron, Pema. 1991. *The Wisdom of no Escape and a Path to Loving Kindness.* USA: Shambala.

Chopra, Deepak. 1993. *Ageless body, Timeless Mind.* New York, USA: Harmony Books.

Cilento, R. 1993. *Heal cancer: Choose your own survival path.* Melbourne, Australia: Hill of Content Publishing Company, Pty Ltd.

Cohen, Misha Ruth, and Kalia Doner. 1996 *The Chinese way to healing: Many paths to wholeness.* USA: The Berkley Publishing Co.

Dalai Lama, Desmond Tutu, Douglas Abrams. 2016. *The Book of Joy— Lasting Happiness in a Changing World.* UK: Penguin Random House.

Dossey, Larry. 1989. *Recovering the soul: A scientific and spiritual search.* New York: Bantam Books.

Dossey, Larry. 1991. *Meaning and Medicine.* New York: Bantam Books.

Dossey, Larry. 1993. *Healing words: The power of prayer and practice of medicine.* New York: Harper-Collins Francisco.

Egan, G. 2002. *The Skilled Helper: A Problem-Management And Opportunity-Development Approach To Helping.* 7th ed. Pacific Grove: Brooks/Cole

Emden, C. and J. Nugent. 1992. *Issues in Australian Nursing 3.* UK: Churchill Livingstone.

Erikson, E.H. 1950. *Childhood and Society.* USA: Norton.

Evans-Wentz, W.Y., Ed. 1960. *The Tibetan Book of the Dead*. UK: Oxford University Press.

Feil, Naomi. 1993. The validation breakthrough: *Simple Techniques for Communicating with People with "Alzheimer's-Type Dementia."* USA: Health Professions Press, Inc.

Feinstein, D., & Eden, D. (2008). Six pillars of energy medicine: Clinical strengths of a complementary paradigm. *Alternative Therapies*, 14(1), 44-54.

Fox, Matthew. 1983. *Original Blessing*. Santa Fe, New Mexico: Bear & Co.

Furth, Greg. 2002. *The Secret World of Drawings—A Jungian Approach to Healing Through Art*. Canada: Inner City Books.

Gawain, Shakti. 1985. *Creative Visualisation*. USA: Bantam Books.

Gawler, Ian. 1984. *You Can Conquer Cancer: Prevention and Management*. Melbourne, Australia: Hill of Content Publishing Company Ltd.

Geary, B., and J. Zeig. 2001. *The Handbook of Ericksonian Psychotherapy*. Phoenix, Arizona: The Milton H. Erickson Foundation Press.

Gibran, Kahlil. 1923. *The Prophet*. London: William Heinemann.

Goldner, Diane. 1999. *How People Heal: Exploring the Scientific Basis of Subtle Energy in Healing*. Charlottesville, Virginia: Hampton Roads Publishing Company, Inc.

Griffiths, Bede. 1982. *The Marriage of East and West*. London: William Collins Sons & Co Ltd.

Harvey, Andrew. 2006 *A Walk with Four Spiritual Guides*. USA: SkyLight.

Hay, Louise. 1987. *You Can Heal Your Life*. USA: Hay House.

Houston, Jean. 1982. *The Possible Person—A Course in Enhancing Your Physical, Mental and Creative Abilities*. California: Jeremy Tarcher Inc.

Jafolla, Mary-Alice. 1982. *The Simple Truth: A Basic Guide to Metaphysics*. Canada: Unity Books Unity Village.

Johnson, R. 1983 *We: Understanding the Psychology of Romantic Love*. New York: Harper and Row.

Johnson, R. 1989. *She: Understanding Feminine Psychology*. Revised Edition. New York: Harper and Row.

Johnson, R. 1989. *He: Understanding Masculine Psychology*. Revised Edition. New York: Harper and Row.

Johnson, Robert. 1991. *Owning Your Own Shadow*. New York: HarperCollins Publishers.

Jung, Carl G. 1969. *Man and His Symbols*. Garden City, NY: Doubleday.

Kehoe, John. 1987. *Mind Power*. West Vancouver, Canada: Zoetic Inc.

Kornfield, Jack. 1994. *A path with Heart—A Guide Through the Perils and Promises of Spiritual Life*. USA: Bantam Books.

Kornfield, Jack. 2000. *After the Ecstasy, The Laundry*. USA Bantam Books.

Krieger, Dolores. 1993. *Accepting Your Power to Heal*. Santa Fe, New Mexico: Bear & Co.

Kübler-Ross, E. 1969. *On Death and Dying*. London: Tavistock.

Kübler-Ross, E. 1979. *The Dougy Letter—A Letter to a Dying Child*. California: Celestial Arts/Ten Speed Press.

Kübler-Ross, Elisabeth. 1975. *Death—The Final Stage of Growth*. New York: Simon & Schuster, Inc.

Kübler-Ross, Elisabeth, and David Kessler. 2001. *Life Lessons: How Our Mortality Can Teach Us About Life and Living*. U.K: Simon & Schuster, Inc.

Kübler-Ross, Elisabeth. 1982. *Living with Death and Dying*. London: Souvenir Press.

Kunz, Dora van Gelder. 1991. *The personal aura*. Wheaton, Illinois: Quest Books.

Lamerton, Richard. 1990, *Care of the Dying*. UK Penguin Books.

Librach, S. Lawrence, and Bruce P. Squires. 1997. The Pain Manual: Principles and Issues in Cancer Pain Management. Montreal, Quebec: Pegasus Healthcare International.

Lugton, Jean, and Margaret Kindlen. 2002. *Palliative Care: The Nursing Role*. Edinburgh, UK: Churchill Livingstone.

Lynn, S., J. Rhue, and I. Kirsch. 2010. *Handbook of Clinical Hypnosis*. Washington DC: American Psychological Association.

Macrae, Janet. 1988. *Therapeutic Touch—A practical Guide*. New York: Alfred A. Knopf, Inc.

Maddocks, Ian. 1997. *Palliative Care: A Study Text*. SA, Australia: The International Institute of Hospice Studies.

Mann, Ivan. 1990. *The Golden Key: Readings and Prayers About Disease and Dying, Life and Hope*. Leicester, UK: Chartwell Press Ltd.

Maslow, Abraham. 1971. *The Farther Reaches of Human Nature*: New York: Viking.

Meares, Ainslie. 1967. *Relief Without Drugs*. UK Souvenir Press Ltd.

Meares, Ainslie. 1993. *The Wealth Within*. Melbourne: Hill of Content.

Mindell, Amy. 1999. *Coma: A Healing Journey—A Guide for Family, Friends, and Helpers*. Portland, Oregon: Lao Tse Press,

Mindell, Arnold. 2010 *Process Mind: A User's Guide to Connecting with the Mind of God*. US: Quest Books.

Mitchell, Emma, Ed. 1998, *Your Body's Energy: A New Approach to Health and Vitality*. Frenchs Forest, NSW: New Holland Publishers Pty Ltd.

Moore, Thomas. 2010. *Care of the Soul in Medicine*. California: Hay House.

Moore, Tony. 1994. *Echoes of the Early Tides: A Healing Journey*. Sydney, Australia: Harper-Collins.

Mount, Balfour M. 1982. *Palliative Care of the Dying, Care for the Dying and Bereaved*. Ed. Ian Gentles. Toronto: Anglican Book Centre.

Mount, Balfour M. 1993. "Whole Person Care: Beyond Psychosocial and Physical Needs." The American Journal for Hospice and Palliative Care, 10 1:28–36.

Moody, R. 1976. *Life After Life*. New York: Bantam Books.

Myss, Caroline. 1999. *The Creation of Health: The Emotional, Psychological, and Spiritual Responses That Promote Health and Healing*. Australia and New Zealand: Transworld Publishers.

Myss, Caroline. 2007. *Entering the Castle—An Inner Path to God and Your Soul*

Omer, Carol. 2015. *Big Girls Little Colouring Book*. US: Beyond Words Publishing Inc.

Orloff, Judith, MD. 2000. *Guide to Intuitive Healing*. New York: Three Rivers Press.

UKRemen, Rachel, N. 1996, *Kitchen Table Wisdom: Stories That Heal*. US: *Riverhead Books.*

Ring, K. 1985. *Heading Towards Omega*. New York: William Morrow.

Rinpoche, Sogyal. 1992. *The Tibetan Book of Living and Dying*. UK: Rider.

Roach, M. Simone, CSM. 1997. *Caring from the Heart: The Convergence of Caring and Spirituality*.USA: Paulist Press.

Saunders, C. 2003. *Watch with Me: Inspiration for a Life in Hospice Care*. Sheffield, UK: Mortal Press.

Schulz, Mona Lisa, and Louise Hay. 2016. *Heal Your Mind: Your Prescription for Wholeness through Medicine, Affirmations, and Intuition*. California: Hay House.

Siegel, Bernie, S. 1998. *Love, Medicine, and Miracles*. US: William Morrow.

Simonton, O. Carl, 1992. *Getting Well Again*. US: Bantam Books.

Sutherland, C. 1992. *Transformed by the Light*. Australia: Bantam Books.

Sutherland, C. 1995. *Children of the Light*. Australia: Bantam Books.

Tacey, David. 2003. *The Spirituality Revolution: The Emergence of Contemporary Spirituality*. Australia: Harper Collins Publishers.

Tolle, Eckhart. 2004. *The Power of Now—A Guide to Spiritual Enlightenment*. Australia: Hodder.

Tolle, Eckhart. 2005. *A New Earth—Create a Better Life*. Australia: Penguin.

Twycross, Robert. 1995. *Introducing Palliative Care*. Oxford, UK: Radcliffe Medical Press.

Vachon M. L. S. W. A. L. Lyall, and S. J. J. Freeman. 1978. "Measurement and Management of Stress in Health Professionals Working with Advanced Cancer Patients." Death Education, 1:365–75, 1978.

Webb, Val. 2002. *Florence Nightingale—The Making of a Radical Theologian*. US: Chalice Press.

Welch, Fern, Rose Winters, and Ken Ross. 2009. *Tea with Elisabeth—Tributes to Hospice Pioneer Dr. Elisabeth Kübler Ross*. US: Quality of Life Publishing Co.

Westburg, Granger, E. 2011. *Good Grief*. US: Fortress Press.

White, John. 1988. *A Practical Guide to Death And Dying*. USA: The Theosophical Publishing House.

Williams, Marjery. n.d. *The Velveteen Rabbit*. New York: Doubleday and Company.

Printed in the United States
By Bookmasters